IBERIAN AND LATIN AMERICAN STUDIES

Galdós's Torquemada *Novels*

IBERIAN AND LATIN AMERICAN STUDIES

Galdós's Torquemada *Novels: Waste and Profit in Late Nineteenth-Century Spain*

TERESA FUENTES PERIS

UNIVERSITY OF WALES PRESS
CARDIFF
2007

British Library Cataloguing-in-Publication Data
A catalogue record for this book is available from the British Library.

ISBN 978–0–7083–2059–4

Typeset by Columns Design Ltd, Reading
Printed and bound in Great Britain by
Antony Rowe Ltd, Chippenham, Wiltshire

To Yolanda

Contents

Contents

Series Editors' Foreword

Over recent decades, the traditional 'languages and literatures' model in Spanish departments in universities in the United Kingdom has been superceded by a contextual, interdisciplinary and 'area studies' approach to the study of the culture, history, society and politics of the Hispanic and Lusophone worlds – categories which extend far beyond the confines of the Iberian Peninsula, not only to Latin America but also to Spanish-speaking and Lusophone Africa.

In response to these dynamic trends in research priorities and curriculum development, this series is designed to present both disciplinary and interdisciplinary research within the general field of Iberian and Latin American Studies, particularly studies which explore all aspects of **Cultural Production** (*inter alia* literature, film, music, dance, sport) in Spanish, Portuguese, Basque, Catalan, Galician and the indigenous languages of Latin America. The series also aims to publish research on the **History and Politics** of Hispanic and Lusophone worlds, both at the level of region and that of the nation-state, as well as on **Cultural Studies** which explore the shifting terrains of gender, sexual, racial and postcolonial identities in those same regions.

Preface

This book addresses the idea of 'waste versus profit' in the four novels of Galdós's *Torquemada* series: *Torquemada en la hoguera* (1889), *Torquemada en la cruz* (1893), *Torquemada en el purgatorio* (1894) and *Torquemada y San Pedro* (1895). At the time these novels were written, discussion of notions of 'profit', 'productivity' and 'utility' was becoming commonplace in intellectual life. These ideas arose from the new ideology of economic liberalism and scientific rationalism which confronted the 'waste' and 'inefficiency' characteristic of pre-modern modes of production.

A feature of this book is the exploration of Galdós's writing in the light of contemporary debates on political economy, public health and social and moral commentary, a methodology which I employed in my previous book, *Visions of Filth: Deviancy and Social Control in the Novels of Galdós* (2003). In this new study I investigate the extent to which notions of profit, efficiency and utility inform the *Torquemada* series by being juxtaposed with contemporary ideas on economic waste, inefficiency and 'loss'. Amongst the various discourses which shape the novels was the discourse on public health, whose agenda ranged from the sanitation of public space to the control of disease. In connection with this, I examine the idea of the recycling of waste, both organic and 'human' – in the case of the latter, the possibility of reforming 'human rejects'. The *Torquemada* novels portray a world in which profit and utility reign supreme, in which not even waste is allowed to go to waste.

Other discourses circulating during the period which also had a profound impact on the *Torquemada* series were the discourse on philanthropy – which coalesced with social commentary on poverty and charity – and that on political economy and the associated idea of utility. Running through all these discourses, which were inevitably intertwined, was the idea of 'waste versus profit', both at *individual* and *national* levels. The discourse on philanthropy, for instance, assumed the attainment of a personal spiritual reward for both parties involved, the philanthropist and the sinner, thereby transforming the philanthropic relationship into a kind of commercial transaction. At a national level, the numerous debates on hygiene and public health revealed anxieties about the waste of human capital represented by disease and racial degeneration, emphasizing consistently the economic value of life and the need to safeguard it in the interests of the health of the nation.

In addressing notions of waste and profit, the book will necessarily draw on a series of interconnected dichotomies – present in both the novels and in contemporary social commentary – which are a variation on the main thematic dichotomy of 'waste versus profit'. These dichotomies are: hygiene (physical and moral) versus poor hygiene; health versus disease; utility versus uselessness; gain (material or spiritual) versus loss; economic productivity versus economic inefficiency; national progress versus national backwardness; thrift versus squander; hard work versus idleness; rational-scientific charity versus indiscriminate, wasteful charity; moral worth versus immorality. The analysis of these issues is appropriate given Galdós's interest in political economy. I will show the ways in which the novels of the *Torquemada* series – firmly anchored in the social, cultural and intellectual contexts of the late nineteenth century – reproduce contemporary debates on 'waste versus profit'. I also intend to identify Galdós's stance and assess his personal contribution to these debates.

In addition to influential sources on political economy emanating abroad, the book makes use of contemporary Spanish sources, in particular the large number of works on hygiene and public health produced at the end of the century, the work of Philippe Hauser being an obvious example. Further sources exploited are contemporary Spanish medical journals (such as *El Siglo Médico*) and conference transactions. In respect of the latter, the transactions of the International Congresses on Hygiene and Demography which took place in the second half of the nineteenth century, particularly those of the meeting held in Madrid in 1898, constitute a crucial source, as they include a series of articles on morbid heredity and degenerative diseases (including meningitis, cretinism and epilepsy), and the effect of these on national efficiency, which help illuminate issues raised by Galdós. Furthermore, the writings of Dr Manuel Tolosa Latour, a close friend of Galdós and a specialist in child hygiene, provides another useful source. (It is significant that Tolosa took part in a number of debates in the International Congress on Hygiene and

Demography held at Madrid.) The work of the contemporary writer and philanthropist Concepción Arenal offers valuable insights with regard to issues of philanthropy and charity. Finally, Galdós's own library, extant in the Casa-Museo Pérez Galdós, Las Palmas de Gran Canaria, includes an important number of works on hygiene and, in particular, on racial degeneration.

I would like to thank the many people who have contributed, in different ways, to the research and writing of this book. I have benefited from the useful comments of a number of scholars, in particular those offered by Christopher Murphy, Nicholas Round and Akiko Tsuchiya. I am especially grateful to Rhian Davies for responding to my queries and being always ready to offer advice and suggestions. My thanks are also extended to other academic colleagues: Richard Cleminson, Elena Delgado, Paul Garner, Jo Labanyi, Alex Longhurst and Patricia McDermott. I should also like to express my gratitude to the staff of various libraries, in particular the library of the Real Academia de Medicina in Madrid (my special thanks here go to Nacho Díaz Delgado-Peñas for his continued professional assistance over the years), the Ateneo of Madrid, the Biblioteca Nacional de España, the Casa-Museo Pérez Galdós (Las Palmas de Gran Canaria) and The British Library. This book would not have been possible without the one-semester sabbatical granted to me by the Department of Spanish and Portuguese, Leeds University, and a matching AHRB study leave award. Finally, my special thanks go to Alistair for his constant support.

Teresa Fuentes Peris
Ilkley, West Yorkshire
January 2006

Introduction

No Room for Waste: the *Torquemada* Novels in the Context of their Age

Critics of Galdós's *Torquemada* novels, in the wake of the trend in criticism that has frequently emphasized Galdós's spiritual tendencies during this period, have tended to concentrate on the author's concerns with religious and moral issues and on the conflict between materialism and spirituality. From this critical perspective, the miser Torquemada has been seen as representative of the spiritual vacuity and the materialistic concerns of late nineteenth-century Spanish society. Scanlon, for instance, has viewed the *Torquemada* novels as Galdós's most 'vigorous indictment' of the materialistic spirit of the age. She writes: 'The central motif of all four novels is the religious–materialistic dichotomy and it is my purpose to attempt to demonstrate how Galdós manipulates this motif in order to underline the inversion of moral values, which he sees as one of the most characteristic features of the society of his day'.[1] The spiritual–material dichotomy has also been emphasized by Folley, who comments that 'the principal concept of the novels [is] the conflict between money and religious values, or, in other words, between Matter and the Spirit'.[2] Similarly, for Schyfter, Torquemada is as a symbolic representation of a false convert who betrays, or is unable to comprehend, the spiritual values necessary in the modern world. Schyfter argues that through Torquemada, who is seen as representing modern man's confusion in a world devoid of faith or direction, Galdós exposes the spiritual deficiencies of nineteenth-century Spain.[3]

Although these studies have in various ways addressed Galdós's focus on materialism, they have not examined it within the framework of waste and profit, in particular, within discourses circulating at the time on political economy, public health and philanthropy. The pervasiveness of debates on utility and profit, as well as notions and images related to waste, in both nineteenth-century commentary and Galdós's *Torquemada* novels, is indicative of the impact that these ideas had on the society of the time. It is my contention that the novels of the *Torquemada* series are not solely an expression of Galdós's spiritual preoccupations during this period, but a reflection of the author's critical engagement with contemporary social debates.[4]

Notions of 'waste versus profit' within the context of Spanish political economy were greatly influenced by the British author Samuel Smiles. His book *Self-Help* (1859), in which he propounds ideas on productive efficiency, hard work, moral duty, industry, energy, perseverance, initiative, thrift, utility and profit (all seen as conducive to social progress and national wealth) found many supporters in Spain.[5] Another important influence in contemporary Spain was the British economist and theoretical jurist, Jeremy Bentham, a promoter of pragmatism, utilitarianism, rationalism, order and efficiency.[6] Torquemada's utilitarian ethic, his preoccupation with economizing and avoiding waste at all costs – whether of *material* or *human* resources – and his vision of himself as the supreme example of the self-made man are worth noting in respect of these ideas, and constitute the main focus of Chapter 1. In connection with the thrift–improvidence polarity, this chapter examines Torquemada's association of work with hygiene and profit, and leisure time with disease and economic loss. As well as the waste of capital represented by non-productive time, a different aspect of waste studied here is the loss of human life. In analysing Torquemada's utilitarian attitude to death, the chapter explores the link drawn by the protagonist between justice, rationality and utility on the one hand, and injustice, irrationality and waste on the other. As we shall see, these ideas are rooted in contemporary philosophical and judicial commentary, as expounded notably by Bentham.

Chapter 2 has political economy as a backdrop and concentrates on contemporary theories on racial degeneration and the

alarm and anxieties sparked by the increase of hereditary degenerative diseases and mortality rates. The waste of human life
through physical and mental degeneration and death, and the
effects this had on the national economy, permeated the writings
of contemporary public health experts. Hygienic discourse, a
major discourse during this period and one that bears heavily on
the novels, drew on political economy, psychiatric discourse and
general social and moral commentary. The utilitarian ethic of the
period is manifested in the texts of public health experts, who,
taking on board new ideas on political economy, assumed the
responsibility for the country's physical, mental and material
health. Their texts promote the idea that the correct application
of physical and moral hygienic principles saved the nation money
by reducing disease, hence preventing the degeneration of the
race.[7] The issue of racial degeneration is one that figures prominently in the *Torquemada* novels. The numerous examples of
physical and mental degeneration in the series, such as cretinism,
meningitis, epilepsy, anaemia, hysteria and suicide, have tended
to be interpreted as symbolic manifestations of the spiritual and
moral decadence of Spanish society. Going beyond this 'spiritual'
reading of the novels, I would like to argue that they need to be
analysed in the light of discourses on racial degeneration that
circulated at the time.

Further to ideas on inefficiency and waste at national and
social levels, Chapter 3 analyses, within the more specific context
of *personal* profit and loss, the links between the free market and
charitable enterprise: the idea of philanthropy as a trade in which
parties are intent on personal gain, whether material or spiritual.
In the last novel of the series, *Torquemada y San Pedro*, both
Torquemada and the ex-missionary Gamborena are seen to pur-
sue their own individual interests. Although a considerable
number of critical studies have been devoted to Torquemada's
lack of spirituality and his profit-making mentality, this particular
issue has not been examined from the perspective of the relationship between the missionary-philanthropist and the sinner. In
connection with the protagonist's eager attempts to benefit from
his 'contract' with Gamborena (the deal being that he will leave a
large portion of his immense fortune to the poor in exchange for
a place in heaven), this chapter explores the emergence of
utilitarian, rational attitudes to charity, exemplified by Torquemada, an issue which has been disregarded by critics of the

novels. The charity theme also links *Torquemada y San Pedro* with the first novel of the series, *Torquemada en la hoguera*, where similar ideas are expressed. As we shall see, Torquemada's utilitarian view of charity and the poor is one in which the contemporary Catholic Church in Spain participated. This reflects the Catholic Church's ability to adapt and re-position itself as a supporter of the new capitalism.[8] The Church was forced to react to a new economic and social environment in which the mentality of self-help and personal improvement was coming to the fore and displacing old beliefs and attitudes towards poverty. The new mentality posited poverty as self-inflicted, derived from innate moral defects. Furthermore, the changes brought about by industrialization and urbanization led to a gradual association of the poor with the emergence of revolutionary socialism, which contained within it the threat of violent protest and resistance. The traditional view of poverty and charity, based on the ancient perception of the destitute as a deferential social grouping resigned to the lot bestowed upon them by Providence, was increasingly replaced by utilitarian, rationalist attitudes, more in accordance with the times.

In respect of the other party to the contract, the ex-missionary, the chapter draws attention to the fact that the energetic, ambitious and enterprising Gamborena resembles the image of the self-made man, albeit one who is engaged in 'spiritual business'. In doing so, it highlights the relationship between philanthropic enterprise and industrial capitalism, which is reflective, once more, of the Catholic Church's proclivity to change its thinking to bring it more into line with the new capitalism.[9] Regarding the ways in which philanthropic control is deployed, an analysis of the philanthropist-sinner relationship, particularly at the sinner's death-bed, exposes philanthropy as being something more than a disinterested altruistic and humanitarian enterprise. The chapter also looks into the parallels between the role of the missionary in non-European, 'uncivilized' countries on the one hand, and that of the philanthropist among alien and marginalized 'primitive' groups in the 'civilized' word on the other. The nineteenth-century philanthropist's aim was the control, reform, or 'recycling' of those social groups perceived as a threat to respectable and 'civilized' bourgeois society. It is ironic, in this respect, that Torquemada, who, as we shall see, is obsessed with recycling waste, should be regarded by bourgeois society as in need of being recycled himself. Throughout the four novels of the series, Galdós depicts a society in which there is no room for waste. Allusions to waste and terms which connote this idea in its various manifestations are rife from the beginning of the series. Torquemada's concern with making the most of everything is emphasized from the moment the character is first introduced in *Torquemada en la hoguera*, in a humorous passage where the narrator refers to Torquemada and his wife as a 'matrimonio sin desperdicio', '[e]lla defendiendo el céntimo en casa para que no se fuera a la calle, y él barriendo para adentro a fin de traer todo lo que pasara'.[10] Here, the idiomatic expression 'barrer para adentro' ('to look after one's interests') can be interpreted literally as meaning that Torquemada did not even allow waste (the sweepings) to go to waste, an idea reinforced by the use of the phrase 'sin desperdicio' in the same sentence. The couple's exaggerated thrift and their obsession with not squandering waste are mocked by the narrator in this passage.[11] This is not the only time that the image of 'barrer para adentro' is used in the series. In one scene in *Torquemada y San Pedro*, Torquemada complains that his sister-in-law is squandering his money, preventing him from economizing. In this passage, Torquemada describes himself as 'un hombre que ha barrido para su casa todo lo que ha podido' ('barrer para su casa' having the same meaning in Spanish as 'barrer para adentro'); on the other hand, Cruz, his prodigal sister-in-law, is appropriately described by Torquemada as 'barriendo para afuera' (*OC*, 1070). To return to the depiction, noted above, of Torquemada and his wife at the beginning of the series, it is ironic that shortly after the narrator of *Torquemada en la hoguera* introduces us to the thrifty couple, he tells us that, apart from the first and the last, all of their children 'se malograron' (*OC*, 907) – the image of waste ('wasted life' in this instance) standing in contrast here to the couple's zeal for economizing. Of course, the most obvious example of waste is the one represented by the death of the genius Valentín and the subsequent birth of Torquemada's degenerate second son, which will be discussed later.

The idea that waste should not be allowed to go to waste links in with the idea of recycling rubbish. At the time, waste was regarded as part of a system of retrieval, conversion and exchange.[12] Public health experts of the period in Spain, as well as in Britain and France, believed that waste (particularly sewage) could be retrieved and made valuable, and there were numerous proposals for converting useless waste into useful matter, or productive capital. A prevalent idea was to turn waste to good use, or, as a contemporary author put it, 'to get rid of [rubbish] usefully'.[13] Contemporaries drew attention in their writings to the economic value of waste. Usefulness, profit and efficiency were equated with hygiene, and constantly contrasted with expenditure, loss, waste and inefficiency. The idea was to make a profit at a minimum cost. The commercial value of waste was noted, for instance, in an article entitled 'Dirty cleanliness', written for the renowned British journal *Household Words*. The paradoxical title of this article is itself illustrative of the contemporary obsession with recycling waste.[14] Another article in the same journal voiced the belief that filth could be converted into wealth, asserting that '[d]irt itself is not gold, though industry may make it so'.[15] These two articles underline the idea that waste – whether rubbish, refuse or sewage – could have profit extracted from it. It is interesting that Charles Dickens, the editor of *Household Words*, wrote an article for his journal about the possible cure and rehabilitation of cretins.[16] This is significant within the context of the contemporary preoccupation with recycling both organic waste and 'human rejects' – those marginal sectors of society, such as alcoholics, prostitutes, beggars, vagrants or the mentally ill, who were perceived as the waste products of civilization. The visualization of these groups as 'drains' on the national economy (they consumed without contributing anything to the nation) led to attempts to reform social 'deviants' with a view to rendering them useful members of society.[17]

As well as highlighting the economic advantages of recycling waste, public health discourses insisted on its hygienic benefits, a parallel being drawn between the interests of hygiene and those of the economy.[18] The contemporary emphasis on the circulation of waste was derived from the belief that in order to prevent infection, rubbish must not be allowed to accumulate: as with money in the capitalist economy, it needed to be kept circulating. In this way waste would become both innocuous to health and economically useful. In accordance with these ideas, stagnation needed to be avoided at all costs, whereas 'flow' was seen as healthy. At the time, the germ theory of disease was yet to be fully disseminated. As well as filth, damp was considered to be a major cause of disease. Because it was associated with dampness and putrid stagnation, water inspired fear and distrust. Although water in itself generated suspicion in terms of its negative effect on health, its movement – the circulation of water – was considered salubrious. It was believed that matter in circulation or in movement was less likely to become corrupted. This explains the importance attached to the elimination of filth through drainage: drains were believed to decrease the dangers of putrid stagnation.[19] From an organicist point of view, the notion that air and fluids should be kept in a permanent state of movement was the result of the impact of William Harvey's discoveries concerning the bodily circulation of blood. The attention given by Alexandre Parent-Duchâtelet, the leading public health expert in drains and prostitution in mid-nineteenth century France, to the efficient functioning of the drainage system and its ventilation reflects his and other doctors' belief that infection resulted mainly from the absence of movement in water and in air.[20]

In respect of the emphasis on the recycling of waste, the introduction of the character of the rag picker, tía Roma, in *Torquemada en la hoguera* is significant. Tía Roma is described 'la trapera de la casa, viejecita que recogía las basuras y los pocos desperdicios de la comida, *ab initio*, o sea, desde que Torquemada y doña Silvia se casaron, y lo mismo había hecho en la casa de los padres de doña Silvia' (*OC*, 922).[21] Tía Roma scavenges on leftovers from Torquemada's and other people's houses. The idea that in Torquemada's house nothing is wasted is repeated a few lines later, when the narrator says that tía Roma 'tenía gran apego a la casa, cuyas barreduras había recogido diariamente durante luengos años' and adds that doña Silvia 'nunca quiso dar a nadie más que a ella los huesos, mendrugos y piltrafas sobrantes' (*OC*, 922).[22] Tía Roma is not the only character in the novel who recycles waste. Silvia and Torquemada himself are said to recycle food tía Roma scavenged from rich houses where she worked, thus becoming scavengers themselves. In a humorous passage, tía Roma rebukes Torquemada for his over-recycling of food: 'una noche, ¿se acuerda?, traje un hueso de jabalí, que lo estuvo usted echando en el puchero seis días seguidos, hasta que se quedó más seco que su alma puñalera' (*OC*, 933). The episode in this first novel of the series, in which Torquemada gives a beggar his old cape instead of the new one, provides another example of Torquemada's recycling of cast-offs.[23] The idea that nothing must be lost or discarded becomes even more relevant later on in the series, when Torquemada conceives the thought of 'resurrecting' the genius Valentín. In a world where profit and utility hold sway, no waste can be afforded: even death is recycled. In this sense, the birth of the degenerate Valentín – a cretin beyond cure – is perhaps Galdós's greatest irony in the series.

Torquemada's pragmatic attitude reflects the utilitarian ethos of the period taken to an extreme. His exaggerated thrifty habits (which stand in contrast with Cruz's conspicuous overspending in the second and, particularly, third novel of the series), his recycling of leftovers and cast-offs, and his obsession with preventing wastage of any kind, are just one of the many manifestations of the contemporary preoccupation with utility and profit. The waste of human capital through degeneration and death is, as we have seen, a dominant issue in the novels. Examples of this are: the sickness and death through meningitis of the genius child Valentín, whose life, in Torquemada's eyes, is wasted before it can become productive; the cretinism of the second Valentín, whose atavic, savage behaviour represents the waste product of a civilized society; and the deaths of Fidela and Rafael, both examples of wasted youth. The wastefulness of Fidela's death – like that of the first Valentín – is stressed by Torquemada, who reiterates the idea that a 'less useful' life should have been taken instead. Her brother Rafael, a victim of nervous disorders related to hysteria, puts an end to his life at the end of *Torquemada en el purgatorio*, adding to the waste of human life in the series. Furthermore, the notion of not wasting a single chance in the pursuit of profit is a key theme in the last novel of the series. Torquemada's long illness – his stomach complaint – is perceived by him as wasted time when he cannot be economically productive. This is compounded by the death of the protagonist at the end of the series. Death prevents Torquemada from fulfilling his project of converting the external debt into internal debt. Torquemada voices his frustration with his inability to carry out his debt conversion project, and regrets the economic loss that this will entail for the nation. The idea of making the most of every opportunity to secure gains is perhaps most clearly illustrated in the novel by the quasi-commercial transaction, in *Torquemada y San Pedro,* in which Torquemada and the priest Gamborena become involved in an attempt to save Torquemada's soul – a supreme example of the utilitarian mentality of the period.

In connection with the utilitarian ethos, it is also my intention to explore the 'give-and-take' spirit dominant at the time: the 'exchange' mentality according to which one only gives in return for a perceived benefit[24] and, similarly, the related idea that one must prove oneself to be deserving of something in order to win it – the idea being that nothing must be given for free, or, in other words, that nothing must be wasted. There are numerous examples of this in the *Torquemada* series, where everything becomes a transaction. The most evident is Torquemada's dealings with God. The give-and-take that Torquemada believes to exist between humans and God is a theme that links the first and last novels of the series. In *Torquemada en la hoguera*, Torquemada expects that Valentín's life will be saved as payment for his good deeds: that is to say, his charity – or rather what he believes to be charity – to the poor. After Valentín's death, he considers himself 'cheated' or 'deceived' by God, who, in his opinion, has failed to keep his side of the deal. When later in the series Torquemada remarries, and his wife Fidela is expecting a child, he firmly believes that Providence will right wrongs and repay him with the birth of another genius. Thus, he is deeply convinced that the unborn child will be a replica of the first Valentín. In *Torquemada y San Pedro*, Torquemada will try once more to make a deal with God: he will leave his riches to the poor in exchange for the salvation of his soul. This time, though, more wary, Torquemada will ask his spiritual mentor, Gamborena, for guarantees that the contract will be honoured. In the same way as Torquemada wants to make sure that his charitable act will not be a 'waste' for him, Gamborena similarly falls prey to this calculating approach: he is not willing to invest any spiritual capital in converting Torquemada without obtaining a profit in return.

As the self-interested and calculating man he is, Torquemada does not mind giving his money to the poor as long as he can make a profit out of it. It should be noted nonetheless that deep down Torquemada regards the poor as dissolute and wasteful and, therefore, as undeserving of his charity. As we shall see, this point is made on several occasions both in *Torquemada en la hoguera* and *Torquemada y San Pedro*, where the author makes clear what Torquemada's real stance is. Torquemada's pragmatic approach to charity and the poor is in keeping with the new scientific, rational and utilitarian ideas on poverty and the distribution of charity, another manifestation of the exchange mentality in the

Torquemada novels. According to the new conception of charity, it was felt that in many instances the poor were *taking* money from society without *giving* society anything in return. This led to the perception of the poor not only as non-productive but also as a drain on the national economy, thereby bestowing on them the label of 'undeserving'. The idea that one had to become deserving of charity was voiced, for instance, by the philosopher Francisco Giner de los Ríos, who defined the 'mendigo' as a man who 'no tiene otra profesión que la de pedir limosna *sin devolver nada a la sociedad a cambio de ella*' (my emphasis).[25] In connection with this, it was suggested that the poor in asylums needed to work – rather than being idle – in return for the benefits received from society. As a contemporary public health expert put it, the 'asilados' needed to '[devolver] a la sociedad el bien que de ella han recibido.'[26] This is reminiscent of Donoso's advice to Torquemada in *Torquemada en la cruz* that he should remarry and produce more children, because, as he says, 'los hijos son la moneda con que se paga a la nación los beneficios que de ella recibimos' (*OC*, 966).

José Donoso, a friend and benefactor of the Aguila family and a supreme representative of industrial capitalism in the series, is, appropriately, the broker in the marriage of Torquemada into the Aguila family, an arrangement which constitutes another example of the exchange mentality of the period. Galdós is eager to stress that the union is, in effect, a business contract from which both parties will benefit. The preparations for the marriage are referred to by Donoso as 'negociaciones' and 'gestiones' (*OC*, 973, 977), and the 'contrayentes' as 'partes contratantes' (*OC*, 977). The business nature of the union is such that Torquemada is kept in the dark to the very last moment as to which of the two Aguila sisters he is to marry. Through the use of humour in this episode, Galdós ridicules the 'arranged marriage' into which Torquemada is essentially coaxed, exposing it as a 'give-and-take' deal: Torquemada gains a wife (and potential offspring) in exchange for rescuing the decadent aristocratic family from penury. Who the wife will be is unimportant, or, as Cruz puts it: 'un detalle' (*OC*, 977). It is noteworthy that here, Donoso's utilitarian approach, criticized by Galdós, surpasses by far that of Torquemada. On occasions in this episode, the protagonist appears as a 'victim' of a plot devised by Donoso (with Cruz's participation), in which he is barely involved. Torquemada is fully aware of the ridiculous situation into which he has been driven, showing his frustration in the face of Donoso's over-calculating and cold approach to his future marriage, and protesting his right to know at least to whom of the two sisters he will be united. Thus, in a humorous passage he tells Donoso: 'Yo creía . . ., vamos . . ., parecía natural [. . .] que lo primero fuera saber cuál es la rama en que a uno le cuelgan' (*OC*, 973). The humour surrounding Torquemada's terrible doubts as to who his future wife will be testifies to the comical and absurd nature of the marriage deal.

As we shall see in following chapters, Torquemada is not the only recipient of the author's criticism. Bailón, Donoso, Gamborena and Cruz, all of them Torquemada's 'mentors' at different stages in the series, are the target of Galdós's even harsher attack. For all his avarice, selfishness and coarse manners, Torquemada is also a victim of authoritarian and manipulative characters. Torquemada's ignorance, gullibility and moral inferiority makes him more susceptible to being moulded and influenced by others, which has the effect of inclining the reader's sympathies towards the miser. In the *Torquemada* series, Galdós extends his satire on the utilitarian spirit of the period, with which various characters engage, to a more general ethical attack on selfish, ruthless and unscrupulous attitudes and actions of some characters, notably Cruz and Gamborena.[27] Torquemada appears particularly hopeless in his dealings with his imperious and domineering sister-in-law, Cruz. In spite of trying to resist her attempts at 'draining' his finances – as he perceives it – Torquemada is totally overwhelmed by the tyranny she imposes on him. Thus, if Torquemada's zeal for economizing is condemned by the author, his message seems to be that Cruz's wasteful depletion of Torquemada's 'resources' is even more censurable. Moreover, the humour that often surrounds Torquemada's obsession with rationalizing everything, succeeds in tempering the author's criticism of his protagonist.

Galdós's criticism of the spirit of utility of the time does not mean that he disregarded modernity and progress, including improvement in economic and social conditions. As a modern man, Galdós endorsed scientific and technological advance as a counter to backward ideas, still prevalent in Spain, which associated materialism with immorality and a lack of spirituality. Galdós did not conceptualize the spiritual as the antithesis of the material. Rather, he was sympathetic to an ethical materialism which he saw as more 'human' than the 'raw', mechanistic materialism of the utilitarian mentality.

NOTES

[1]   Geraldine M. Scanlon, 'Torquemada: "Becerro de oro"', *Modern Language Notes*, 91 (1976), 264–76, 264–5.

[2]   Terence T. Folley, 'Some considerations of the religious allusions in Pérez Galdós' *Torquemada* novels', *Anales Galdosianos*, XIII (1978), 41–8, 45.

[3]   Sara E. Schyfter, *The Jew in the Novels of Benito Pérez Galdós* (London: Tamesis, 1978). Along these lines, Gustavo Correa (*El simbolismo religioso en las novelas de Pérez Galdós* [Madrid: Gredos, 1962], p. 135) has seen Torquemada as a 'personaje que encarna la antítesis de la criatura religiosa', whereas for Peter G. Earle ('Torquemada: hombre-masa', *Anales Galdosianos*, II [1967], 29–43) Torquemada represents an 'ejemplo culminante [. . .] de la desolación espiritual' (29). Other scholars who have taken a similar critical stance and have stressed the spiritual dimensions of the *Torquemada* series are: William M. Sherzer, 'Death and succession in the *Torquemada* series', *Anales Galdosianos*, XIII (1978), 33–9; Paula W. Shirley, 'Religious contexts in the Torquemada novels', *Hispanófila*, 29, 2 (1986), 67–73; B. J. Zeidner Bäuml, 'The mundane demon: The bourgeois grotesque in Galdós's *Torquemada en la hoguera*', *Symposium* XXIV (Summer 1970), 158–65; and Mac Gregor O'Brien, 'Las religiones de Torquemada', *Discurso Literario*, 9, 2 (1985), 111–19. From this critical perspective Torquemada appears at the opposite pole to profoundly religious characters like Nazarín, Benina or Leré (from the novels *Nazarín* [1895], *Misericordia* [1897] and *Angel Guerra* [1890–91] respectively), all products of Galdós's so-called 'spiritual period'.

[4]   I have made this argument in connection with other novels written by Galdós in the 1890s, which have traditionally been seen as fundamentally spiritual in focus. *Angel Guerra*, for instance, which was written between 1890 and 1891 (significantly covering the period between the production of *Torquemada en la hoguera* and the other three novels of the series) has been studied from the perspective of its protagonist's Tolstoyan religiosity. Similarly, *Nazarín* (1895), *Halma* (1895) and *Misericordia* (1897) have tended to be regarded as a reflection of Galdós's spiritual tendencies and often, as forming part of a trilogy. I have argued that these texts, like the novels of the *Torquemada* series, are also part of contemporary social debates. See Teresa Fuentes Peris, *Visions of Filth: Deviancy and Social Control in the Novels of Galdós* (Liverpool: Liverpool University Press, 2003).

[5]   An abridged Spanish version appeared in 1876 entitled *Los hombres de energía y coraje: Notas biográficas tomadas del popular libro titulado 'Self-Help'*. This version only reproduces one of the chapters of the

original book (ch. 8), entitled 'Energy and Courage'. A full translation of the English version was to appear at a later date (¡*Ayúdate!*
[Barcelona: Ramón Sopena]. Tr. by G. Nuñez de Prado). Although
this version is undated, it was published in 1885 or after, as it contains
the translation of a prologue by Smiles of this date.

6   In fact, the majority of works that had had an impact on the Europe
of the Enlightenment had been translated into Spanish and had
been influential among Spanish intellectual circles during the nineteenth century: as noted by Pedro Trinidad Fernández, 'La reforma
de las cárceles en el siglo XIX: las cárceles de Madrid', in *Estudios de
Historia Social*, 22–3 (1982), 69–187, 88. Bentham not only inspired
the new Penal Codes that were drawn up throughout liberal and
enlightened Europe, he also designed a project for a model prison –
the Panopticon – the plan of which spread throughout Europe, an
efficient and economic instrument for the exercise of power, which
would serve as a model for some penal establishments built from the
end of the eighteenth century. Moreover, as Bentham himself
observed, the surveillance and disciplinary elements of the panopticon scheme could be transferred to the wider social domain, that is,
they could be applied to any social setting in which a particular form
of behaviour had to be imposed, such as asylums, factories, and
schools: see Jeremy Bentham, *The Panopticon; or, the Inspection-House*
(1791), in John Bowring (ed.), *The Collected Works of Jeremy Bentham*
(Edinburgh, 1843), IV, pp. 39–172. The panopticon project constitutes an expression of Bentham's love for order and efficiency both
in the penal and social orders.

7   Hygiene, which requires the exercise of duty and moral rectitude,
was associated in their writings with morality, order and economic
growth. According to the public health expert Angel Fernández
Caro: 'La Higiene [. . .] más que ciencia es un código de moral': see
*Los deberes de la sociedad ante los intereses de la Higiene. Discursos leídos en
la sesión inaugural del año académico de 1886–1887 en la Sociedad
Española de Higiene, celebrada el día 27 de noviembre de 1886* (Madrid:
Imprenta de Enrique Teodoro, 1886), pp. 3–43, 21. Similarly to
utilitarian writers, such as Smiles and Bentham, hygienists subscribed
to the idea that moral order was essential for economic growth.

8   See, in this respect, José Antonio Portero, *Púlpito e ideología en la
España del siglo XIX* (Zaragoza: Libros Pórtico, 1978), esp. pp. 189–
216.

9   Protestant and Catholic conceptions of philanthropic work drew
closer to each other with the emergence of industrial capitalism.
Portero (esp. pp. 189–216) has noted the adaptability of the
Church's ideology to the new capitalist attitudes towards the work
ethic, individual and social progress and wealth, which differed
significantly from pre-modern views on these matters. An obvious
example of this is the episode, in *Torquemada en el purgatorio*, in which
Church representatives come to congratulate Torquemada on his
famous speech – a eulogy of the utilitarian virtues of self-help, hard
work and the pursuit of wealth.

¹⁰ Benito Pérez Galdós, *Obras completas*, 4th edn, vol. 5, ed. by Federico
    Carlos Sainz de Robles (Madrid: Aguilar, 1965), p. 907. In future
    references, *Obras completas* will appear in the text as *OC*, followed by
    the page number.
¹¹ The humour is accentuated by his description of Torquemada and
    his wife as a 'pareja que podría servir de modelo a cuantas hormigas
    hay debajo de la tierra y encima de ella' (*OC*, 907). The mocking
    praise of the couple's exaggerated hard work habits is stressed in
    another passage in which the narrator notes that Torquemada and
    his wife had lived 'en santa y *laboriosa* paz durante más de cuatro
    lustros' (*OC*, 907 [my emphasis]).
¹² Lynda Nead, *Myths of Sexuality: Representations of Women in Victorian
    Britain* (Oxford: Basil Blackwell, 1990), p. 121.
¹³ 'Dirty Cleanliness', *Household Words*, XVIII (24 July 1858), 121–3, 122.
¹⁴ Ibid., 122. The profits that could be drawn from waste are empha-
    sized in a passage where the author asserts that 'the present and
    future generations are and will be witness to the fact of the sweeper's
    buying the sweepings which he was once paid to sweep, and of
    removing them at his own expense' (123).
¹⁵ 'A way to clean rivers', *Household Words*, XVIII (10 July 1858), 79–82,
    80.
¹⁶ See *Household Words*, VII (4 June 1853), 313–17.
¹⁷ It is noteworthy that the issue of how to reuse rubbish was an
    important one in the International Congresses of Hygiene and
    Demography, which took place in the second half of the nineteenth
    century and early twentieth century, and whose main concern was
    the problem of the degeneration of the race.
¹⁸ In 'Dirty Cleanliness', its author expressed anxieties about the over-
    accumulation of residues and sewage waters in the river Thames, as it
    prevented the free flow of the water, and stressed the need to drain
    the waste away. Also, in 'A way to clean rivers', the author put forward
    a series of plans for recycling sewage so that it did not accumulate
    and pollute rivers. He highlighted the economic advantages of this
    plan, propounding the use of the sewage waters in agriculture. In
    Spain, the well-known public health expert Philippe Hauser (*Madrid
    bajo un punto de vista médico-social*, 2 vols [Madrid: Establecimiento
    Tipográfico Sucesores de Rivadeneyra, 1902], vol. 1, pp. 193–7), who
    devoted a chapter of his book to the Madrid drainage system,
    similarly proposed the use of 'aguas fecales' for agricultural pur-
    poses, emphasizing the hygienic and economic advantages of this
    project and the good results obtained from it in other European
    countries. Another issue which concerned hygienists of the period
    was that of domestic rubbish deposited in the streets. In a chapter of
    his book called 'Saneamiento de la vía pública', Hauser significantly
    observed that the IX International Congress on Hygiene and Demog-
    raphy held in Madrid (1898) nominated a committee to study the
    ways of dealing with this problem, which Hauser regarded as vital
    'tanto bajo el punto de vista de la higiene urbana, como de economía
    social' (pp. 199–200). That Hauser includes a table of rubbish tips in

Madrid, specifying to which use rubbish will be put, is illustrative of the importance accorded to the recycling of rubbish both from a hygienic and economic point of view. It is worth noting that these concerns became increasingly popular after the last novel of the series was published in 1895, something which highlights how advanced – one might even say 'modern' – Galdós was in his thinking.

19 Alain Corbin, 'Commercial sexuality in nineteenth century France: A system of images and regulations', in Catherine Gallagher and Thomas Laqueur (eds), *The Making of the Modern Body: Sexuality and Society in the Nineteenth Century* (Berkeley and Los Angeles: University of California Press, 1987), pp. 209–19, 211; and Charles Bernheimer, *Figures of Ill Repute: Representing Prostitution in Nineteenth-Century France* (Cambridge, Mass.: Harvard University Press, 1989), pp. 15–16.

20 Corbin, 'Commercial sexuality', p. 211. Corbin has also noted Parent-Duchâtelet's fascination with the recycling of waste. See, in this respect, his introduction to the abridged edition of the French hygienist's book, written in 1836, *Alexandre Parent-Duchâtelet: La Prostitution à Paris au XIX Siècle* (Paris: Seuil, 1981), pp. 9–41.

21 Hauser has emphasized this point in his study of the role of the *traperos* of Madrid, on which he wrote a whole section of a chapter. He notes that the function of *traperos* is twofold, as they act as both scavengers (collecting and recycling rubbish) and rag pickers (selling, or trafficking with rubbish). Unlike in other European capitals, where *traperos* were only authorized by the municipality to expurgate rubbish from domestic containers, in Madrid they had an authorization to collect the rubbish from containers and carry it in special carriages to rubbish tips, thereby contributing to the municipal management of urban hygiene. See *Madrid bajo un punto de vista médico-social*, vol. 1, pp. 208–10.

22 Jo Labanyi (*Gender and Modernization in the Spanish Realist Novel* [Oxford: Oxford University Press, 2000], pp. 118–21) has observed that the figure of the rag picker occupied a special place in the nineteenth-century social imagination, as new industrial technologies for the recycling of rubbish emerged. Rag pickers, Labanyi argues, were perceived to be necessary to both the public health system, as they prevent rubbish from accumulating, and the economic system, as they keep goods in circulation.

23 Another example of Torquemada's obsession with recycling cast-offs is provided by the scene in *Torquemada en el purgatorio* in which, showing disapproval towards Cruz's over-consumption, he comments that he would prefer to be dressed by 'un sastre habilidoso, de esos que vuelven la ropa del revés' (*OC*, 1075). Similarly, in *Torquemada en la cruz*, Torquemada suggests to the horrified Cruz that she and Fidela might wish to have the diseased Doña Silvia's clothes altered to fit them (*OC*, 1012–13).

24 During this period the exchange mentality was enhanced by the rise of the market economy. Although an exchange economy had existed since antiquity (if not before) as a means of subsistence, it clearly

intensified with the rise of industrial capitalism. With the move away from a pre-modern, closed economy, reflected in an increased circulation of goods and money, economic progress occurred. Transactions increased, and in this highly charged 'exchange economy', individuals increasingly became economic agents, aware of their position in the market place and seeking to maximize personal utility and profit.

25 'La prohibición de la mendicidad y las Hermanitas de los Pobres', *Boletín de la Institución Libre de Enseñanza*, 5 (1881), 49–50, 49.

26 Francisco Javier Santero, *Elementos de higiene privada y pública*, 2 vols (Madrid: El Cosmos, 1985), vol. 2, p. 216.

27 An obvious example of this is Cruz, a patently materialistic and selfish character but one who is depicted as emphatically non-productive. Also, she has no concept of thrift: her conspicuous extravagance is indeed notorious in the series. Similarly, Galdós's criticism of Gamborena's subscription to ideas on utility and profit can be said to be a key part of a broader ethical critique of the priest's self-interested, ruthless and mercenary mentality.

Chapter One

Gain and Loss: Torquemada and the Utilitarian Ethos

One predominant aspect of the *Torquemada* series is the portrayal of its protagonist as the embodiment of a spirit of 'utility and profit', a concept arising from the new ideology of economic liberalism that challenged the 'waste' and 'inefficiency' that was perceived to be associated with the pre-modern economy. Torquemada sees himself, foremost, as the perfect self-made man, energetic, hard working, persevering and thrifty. Particular emphasis is placed by Galdós on the protagonist's championing of the ethic of work and individual effort as contributing to economic and social progress. Throughout the series, the protagonist extols industry and economy, consistent with ideas of the time. This chapter first explores contemporary ideas on self-help and individual achievement, and how Galdós parodies Torquemada's endorsement of the notion of self-help and the figure of the self-made man. It then moves on to analyse, also in connection with the profit–loss polarity, Torquemada's obsession with preventing the waste of *material* and *human* resources, that is to say, the squandering of wealth and human life. An analysis is made of the association drawn by the protagonist between work, utility and good hygiene on the one hand, and idle leisure time, waste and poor hygiene on the other – in keeping with ideas voiced by contemporary public health experts equating hygiene with productivity and profit, and poor hygiene and disease with economic loss. The link established by Torquemada between hygiene and work also leads him to associate the city, where he can be productive, with hygiene, and the countryside with miasmas. Another aspect of waste that this chapter addresses is 'wasted life' and, linked to this, Torquemada's utilitarian approach to death. In this regard, it examines the association of justice with rationality and utility on the one hand, and that of injustice with arbitrariness, illogicality and waste on the other – an association established both in contemporary social commentary and in the novels analysed.

This chapter also attempts to show that Galdós's criticism of extreme utilitarian thought is not directed only against Torquemada, who on occasions appears as a naive recipient of others' ideas. The shallow and pompous Bailón, who becomes Torquemada's advisor in spiritual and worldly matters in *Torquemada en la hoguera*, is presented as the standard-bearer of modern ideas on hygiene. Similarly, Donoso, who replaces Bailón in his role of mentor to the protagonist in the second and third novels of the series (*Torquemada en la cruz* and *Torquemada en el purgatorio*), is portrayed as the supreme representative of industrial capitalism, as the spokesman for economic progress and national wealth. Both Bailón's zeal for hygiene and Donoso's excessive emphasis on utility and material advancement are mocked by the author.

Torquemada: the Self-Made Man

In *Torquemada en el purgatorio*, and particularly in the acclaimed speech Torquemada delivers at the banquet given in his honour, Torquemada advertises himself as the epitome of the 'self-made man', someone who, even if born into the lowest of classes, can succeed in life through hard work, thrift and perseverance. Ideas on self-help were famously propounded in Britain by Samuel Smiles, whose work *Self-Help* (1859) celebrates the values associated with the 'gospel of work'. Smiles firmly believed that the solution to the afflictions and hardships of poverty lay in the individual's hands. In *Self-Help* he produced a long list of brief biographies of self-made men (scientists, merchants, industrialists, artists, writers and workers of all kinds) whose achievements in life were to serve as a model and inspiration for others. The majority of these were of humble origins and, in spite of the difficulties that many of them encountered in the course of their working lives, they rose out of their poverty and improved their social position in life through industry, energy, determination and individual initiative, virtues that Smiles stressed constantly throughout the pages of his book. The first chapter of *Self-Help* opens with the maxim: 'Heaven helps those who help themselves'.[1] In *Self-Help*, Smiles contrasts the moral attributes of the self-made man with the immorality of the idle and the improvident, drawing a link between profit, utility, efficiency and moral worth on the one hand, and waste, uselessness and moral degradation on the other. Smiles was eager to emphasize the social and national benefits of individual betterment: the self-made man's usefulness to his fellow men and to society at large. He highlighted the impact of individual action and personal development on the power and wealth of the nation. As he observed: 'national progress is the sum of individual industry, energy and uprightness, as national decay is of individual idleness, selfishness and vice'.[2] Smiles's catalogue of individual and social virtues and vices, it has been noted, reflected the needs of a society in which, in spite of industrial progress, there were still large areas of waste and inefficiency.[3] Smiles condemned both *individual* and *social* waste and encouraged self-advancement through industry and perseverance.

The message of *Self-Help* spread rapidly and widely. As Briggs puts it: 'Cholera itself could have travelled no faster'.[4] But Smiles was not the only commentator who championed the doctrine of work and self-advancement. In both Europe and the United States, the middle and late nineteenth century saw a large output of 'success' literature which aimed to convey a moral message as well as advice on how to survive and 'get on' in an increasingly industrialized, capitalist society.[5] Although the ideas found in *Self-Help* were common at the time, Smiles's book had a greater and longer-lasting impact than other books of its kind.[6] The impact of Smiles's ideas in Spain was significant. Rafael María de Labra, a renowned Krausist,[7] in a speech given at the Ateneo Mercantil of Madrid in 1878, praised individual action and initiative, drawing a link between personal effort and material progress. He exhorted his audience: 'tened muy en cuenta que nada tan valioso para los pueblos, para las sociedades, como el avivamiento de la fuerza individual, de la iniciativa individual. Después de todo, el individuo es de donde la sociedad saca sus medios, su vigor, su riqueza'. Labra goes on to say that: 'en la dignidad, la inteligencia y el vigor del individuo, del ciudadano, están la bienandanza, el brillo y el porvenir de la sociedad'.[8] Like Smiles, Labra associated progress and civilization with moral fibre, or 'adelantamiento moral'. Similarly, Valentín Morán, in his 1879 inaugural speech to the 'Conferencias para obreros', organized by the Sociedad Económica Matritense (of which Morán was the secretary), associated self-help and individual enterprise with national progress and morality. Morán's speech reads like a 'micro' version of Smiles's *Self-Help.* He provides a long series of examples of working men (both from Spain and Western Europe) who rose to fame through personal initiative, constant application to work and tenacity. In the same way as Smiles, Morán emphasized the impact of individual development on national growth, drawing attention to what these men achieved, not only for themselves, but also for the benefit of their countries and for human progress.[9]

Work, and more specifically the work ethic, came increasingly to be seen the basis for productive efficiency and national wealth. Smiles, making a eulogy of the virtues of hard work, asserted:

> Honourable industry travels the same road with duty, and Providence has closely linked both with happiness. [. . .] By labour the earth has been subdued, and man redeemed from barbarism; nor has a single step in civilization been made without it. Labour is not only a necessity and a duty, but a blessing: only the idler feels it to be a curse.[10]

Utilitarians, especially John Mill, had similarly equated actions of hard work with a 'higher' pleasure that delivered long-term happiness; this was different from sensual pleasures, for example, that produced short-term, 'lower' pleasure, which could lead to 'negative utility' and unhappiness.[11] In *Character* (1871),[12] where Smiles devoted a whole chapter to the virtues of work, he stressed its importance in character building. As he observed, work teaches method, diligence, perseverance, foresight, moral discipline and independence. Methodical work also inculcates notions of economy, as it teaches the individual to use discretion in his/her management of time. The idea of work as a source of wealth had previously been proposed by Bentham, whose utilitarian philosophy had an influence on Smiles. As a good bourgeois utilitarian, Bentham was prompted by the principle of interest and benefit. He argued in favour of the use of work in prisons as an instrument of reform, and organized it as if it were a private, profit-making enterprise. Penitentiaries were conceived by him as schools for the making of *useful* members of society. The principles of Bentham's panopticon model were seen in other disciplinary, or 'carceral' institutions, where built-form and strict regimes of conduct aimed to inculcate efficiency and a general ethic of improvement. During the nineteenth century, both in Spain and elsewhere in Europe, work was the main instrument of order and discipline in prisons, and in other institutions where control needed to be imposed, such as lunatic asylums and *casas de beneficencia*.

In Torquemada's famous speech, delivered at the banquet held to celebrate his sponsoring of the building of a railway line, Galdós demonstrates the impact that these ideas had in Spain. The speech, which enshrines the utilitarian virtues of hard work, individual effort and personal initiative – all of which were seen to lead to material progress and national wealth – constitutes a mockery of Torquemada's ideas on self-help and the perception of himself as a typical example of a self-made man. Its serious intent is shrouded in humorous remarks from the very beginning, when Torquemada is shown trying to impress his audience through the repetition of refined expressions he had learnt from Donoso and through the use of sentences and terms he had either heard at the Senate or read in the newspapers.[13] The narrator stresses the linguistic hurdles the orator comes across, how he gets confused ('se embarulla') and manages to get out of the 'laberintos' he creates for himself. Torquemada's attempts at using elevated diction throughout have a comical effect which cannot be ignored and which reinforce Galdós's parody of Torquemada's vision of himself as a self-made man.[14]

Torquemada indeed introduces himself to his audience as the embodiment of Smiles's self-made man: as someone who, in spite of his humble origins, has risen to a position of usefulness in life through his initiative, industry, perseverance and honesty. Thus he describes himself as 'un pobre obrero, un hombre que todo se lo debe a su misma iniciativa, a su laboriosidad, a su honradez, a su constancia' (*OC*, 1099); and he goes on to say:

> Nací, como quien dice, en la mayor indigencia, y con el sudor de mi rostro he amasado mi pan, y he vivido, *orillando* un día y otro día las dificultades, cumpliendo siempre mis obligaciones y *evacuando* mis negocios con la más estrictísima moralidad. [. . .] Si he llegado a donde estoy, lo debo a que he tenido dos virtudes [. . .]: el trabajo, la conciencia. (*OC*, 1099)[15]

Later in the speech he proclaims, in a self-satisfied manner: '¿Queréis que *os defina mi actitud* moral y religiosa? Pues sabed que mis dogmas son el trabajo, la honradez [. . .], el amor al prójimo y las buenas costumbres'; and congratulating himself on his self-reliance he continues: '[d]e estos principios parto yo siempre, y por eso he podido llegar a labrarme una posición independiente' (*OC*, 1101). The virtues that Torquemada boasts coincide with those which, according to Smiles, a self-made man should possess. The irony is that Torquemada has succeeded in life at the expense of the poor. Thus, the fact that he takes pride in having emerged from poverty and made progress in life through hard work and individual initiative makes the image that he intends to portray of himself as a self-made man laughable. Even more laughable, if not pitiful, is the fact that in his speech, as we have just seen, he promotes honesty as a factor of his individual success, and claims to have always been charitable and benevolent with his fellow human beings (*OC*, 1099).[16] One of the fundamental virtues of the self-made man as conceptualized by Smiles was, in fact, moral fibre. In Smiles's view, elevation of character and moral worth was more important than material prosperity and worldly success. In this respect, he advocated courtesy and benevolence, and warned against selfishness, cruelty, an unforgiving nature and lack of respect for the feelings of others.[17] The fact that Torquemada is shown to display the character traits deplored by Smiles adds to Galdós's mockery of the protagonist's perception of himself as an exemplary self-made man: Torquemada would hardly deserve a place among Smiles's heroes of self-help.

Torquemada's sense of his moral worth derives from the fact that he regards himself essentially as a hard-working man: 'Soy un individuo [. . .] *eminentemente* trabajador' (*OC*, 1099), he announces. Echoing ideas voiced by contemporaries, including public health experts, philanthropists and commentators on moral and social issues, Torquemada associates hard work with moral rectitude, while condemning idleness as the lowest of vices. Against idleness and other vices, Torquemada promotes a pragmatic spirit in terms of industry, profit and utility – in line with the rationalism that was beginning to characterize industrialization. As a hard-working individual and a man of action he claims that he has never encouraged idleness ('como trabajador, *por excelencia*, nunca, nunca he *dado pábulo* a la ociosidad ni he protegido a gente viciosa'), as in his view, 'eso [. . .] ya no sería caridad ni humanidad, sino falta de sentido práctico; eso sería *dar el mayor de los pábulos* a la vagancia' (*OC*, 1100). Torquemada's tirade against idleness ends with a humorous note, as he declares boastfully: 'De mí se podrá decir todo lo que se quiera; pero no se dirá nunca que he sido el Mecenas de la holgazanería' (*OC*, 1100).

The equation of idleness with moral degradation needs to be understood within the context of contemporary beliefs in respect of poverty, begging and charity. In the new industrial order, the deferential figure of the poor as a mere passive recipient of the charity of the wealthy no longer had a reason to exist and, similarly, the Christian duty of aiding the poor became replaced by the need to inculcate them with the values of the new industrialized society. In keeping with these ideas, it was felt that beggars and vagrants should be swept up from the streets and secluded in *asilos* or *casas de beneficencia*, which had been created to instil the ethic of work in beggars. The aim of these projects of reform was to recycle 'human rejects' into a useful and productive workforce. In this context of political economy, charity was essentially a utilitarian enterprise. As we shall see in Chapter 3, Torquemada is shown in the series to regard charity as wasteful because in his view the poor are idle and dissolute, and any money given to them would invariably be drunk or gambled away. In accordance with ideas of the time, he sees charity as breeding idleness and immorality. When in *Torquemada y San Pedro* Gamborena advises Torquemada that in order to save his soul he should remember the poor in his will, and that it is unjust that he should possess so much wealth when others have nothing, Torquemada replies: 'Total, que hay muchos, muchísimos pobres. Yo también he sido pobre. Si ahora soy rico, a mí mismo me lo debo' (*OC*, 1178). During this period, notions of individual worth and personal betterment had begun to displace old attitudes and beliefs about poverty. Alongside the new economic thinking, which emphasized the free market and the free operation of the self-interested individual, the notion grew that poverty was self-inflicted. Increasingly it was believed that the poor were destitute because of their intrinsic moral corruption. The inference of Torquemada's words in the above passage seems to be that the situation in which the poor find themselves and their failure in life is a function of their own nature, reflecting contemporary beliefs.

Torquemada's belief that each person is a product of his/her own actions is in keeping with his perception of himself as a self-made man. The utilitarian idea that through hard work, energy and perseverance one could escape a life of poverty, and that a high position in life could only be achieved through one's individual efforts, is reiterated throughout the pages of *Self-Help*. Torquemada's emphasis on individual enterprise and achievement, in line with the workings of *laissez-faire* economics, echoes the self-interested individualism of the period. The competitive struggle that characterized industrial capitalism celebrated personal success and advancement; conversely, it also placed in sharp relief the link between personal failure and individual vice. This was an emergent system of values consistent with contemporary social Darwinist thought – that is, it mapped the theory of the 'survival of the fittest' in the physical environment onto human behaviour in the social domain.[18] Torquemada voices these views when he declares:

> He partido siempre del principio de que cada cual es dueño de su propio destino; y será feliz el que sepa labrarse su felicidad y desgraciado el que no sepa labrársela. No hay que quejarse de la suerte . . . ¡Oh la suerte: pamplinas, tontería, *dilemas, antinomias, maquiavelismos!* No hay más desgracias que las que uno se *acarrea* con sus yerros. Todo el que quiere poseer los *intereses* materiales no tiene más que buscarlos. (*OC,* 1100)[19]

Torquemada's words stress the notion that personal success is purely an individual responsibility, hence ascribing failure in life to weakness of character. Continuing this line of thought, he dismisses bad luck as the cause of individual failure (*OC,* 1100). Torquemada proclaims that '[l]a suerte protege al que trabaja' (*OC,* 946), which resembles Smiles's ideas on fortune. As he observed in *Self-Help*: 'Fortune is usually on the side of the industrious, as the winds and the waves are on the side of the best navigators'.[20] With regard to Torquemada's views on fortune, both humour and the misuse of terms by him undermine his pronouncements on the issue.

It can be argued that Galdós not only parodies Torquemada's vision of himself as the embodiment of the self-made man, but also draws attention to the flaws associated with the concept of self-help and the image of the self-made man. In spite of the fact

that in Galdós's journalistic works there is an explicit endorsement of hard work, independence and self-help to combat the
effects of self-imposed poverty and the passive resignation to one's
lot in life[21] (something that is also suggested in his fictional works
of the 1880s and 1890s),[22] Galdós was aware that self-help and the
ethic of work were far from being practical and realistic solutions
to the problem of poverty. In the *Torquemada* series, by presenting
a character who achieves social status and prosperity at the
expense of the poor, Galdós highlights the ideal nature of the
notion of the self-made man as conceived by Smiles and promoted by his followers: for somebody born into poverty it is not
easy to ascend socially in life by honest means. Galdós's message
seems to be that personal initiative and perseverance are not
wholly sufficient to succeed in life.[23] By discarding the notion that
the poor are agents of their own misfortune, Galdós is implicitly
disagreeing with his protagonist's perception that *all* the poor are
'undeserving'.[24]

The quasi-caricature of Torquemada as a self-made man is
reinforced by the protagonist's perception of himself as a model
of thrift. As with the ethic of work, thrift was publicized by
middle-class commentators and associated with moral rectitude
and respectability. Thrift was seen as crucial not only for the
material progress of the working classes, but also for their moral
enrichment. National progress would inevitably proceed, it was
envisioned, from the improvement in working-class morals and
economic conditions. *La Voz de la Caridad*, a journal edited by the
writer and philanthropist Concepción Arenal, ran a large number
of articles on thrift and on how to encourage it among the
working classes.[25] Thrift was, indeed, extolled as a paramount
virtue of the self-made man and as a basis of self-help. Economy
was, according to Smiles, 'the exhibition of self-help in one of its
best forms'.[26] He proposed 'the practice of simple economy' as a
way to secure independence, and attacked individual waste and
improvidence.[27] Economy was equated with 'order [. . .] [,]
management, regularity, prudence, and the avoidance of waste'.
As Smiles put it: 'The spirit of economy was expressed by our
Divine Master in the words: "Gather up the fragments that
remain, so that nothing may be lost"'.[28] This is reminiscent of
Torquemada's attitude towards cast-offs: his obsession with not
allowing waste to go to waste. Here, Galdós may be criticizing
these extreme utilitarian ideas. Nonetheless, it should be noted

that although Smiles promoted economy in contrast to improvidence and useless expenditure, he disapproved of thrift taken to an extreme, and condemned those who avoided spending out of avarice. His contempt for miserly individuals is reflected in his assertion that: '[t]hrift is not in any way connected with avarice, usury, greed or selfishness. It is in fact the very reverse of these disgusting dispositions'.[29]

Countering these ideas, a different current of opinion proposed that under-consumption (a possible consequence of thrift) was responsible for the underemployment of capital and labour, hence having a negative impact on national progress and economic growth.[30] In *Torquemada en la cruz*, Donoso acts as the vehicle for these ideas. In his view, Torquemada's excessive thrift (his 'sobriedad sórdida', as he puts it) is a sin against society: it does not contribute to economic and national prosperity since it prevents the flow of capital. According to Donoso, money needs to be invested, that is, put into circulation for it to become productive. This is, in his opinion, a social duty of the rich.[31] As we shall see in Chapter 2, the notion that one should put society's well-being before individual pursuits, and that as an individual one has duties to the community, was deeply ingrained in contemporary thought.[32] Thus, Donoso advises Torquemada:

> cada cual debe vivir en armonía con sus posibles, y así tiene derecho a exigirlo la sociedad. [. . .] Si el pudiente vive cubierto de harapos, ¿me quiere usted decir cómo ha de prosperar la industria? Pues y el comercio, ¿me quiere usted decir cómo ha de prosperar? ¡Adiós riqueza de las naciones, adiós movimiento mercantil, adiós cambios, adiós belleza y comodidad de las grandes capitales, adiós red de caminos de hierro! . . . (*OC*, 958–9)

Later in the series, and simultaneously with his social ascension, Torquemada leaves behind his petit usury habits and, under the influence and advise of Donoso, who introduces him to the world of high finance, he begins to invest his money on a large scale, hence becoming 'useful' to the nation.[33] It needs to be noted, however, that although after his marriage into the Aguila family Torquemada is forced to abandon his sordid habits of usury, he will continue to advocate economy, deploring Cruz's useless expenditure.

In his speech, Torquemada is shown to have absorbed Donoso's teachings, as he draws the audience's attention to his altruistic nature, or, put in other words, to his 'usefulness' to the community. Torquemada believes that by sponsoring 'los grandes adelantos del siglo' – namely, the construction of a railway line – (*OC*, 1101), he is looking after the general interest of humanity. He declares: 'Yo no miro a mi interés, sino al interés general, al interés público de la Humanidad' (*OC*, 1101). This idea is reinforced when he asserts: 'no acaricio más idea que el bien de mi patria' (*OC*, 1102), deceiving himself into believing that he is serving the community's interests rather than self-interest. Later in the series, in *Torquemada y San Pedro*, when Gamborena tries to make Torquemada confess his avarice before his death, the latter is not convinced by Gamborena's belief that his plan to convert the foreign debt into a domestic one is sinful, that is to say, dictated by his avarice. Guided by Donoso's doctrine, Torquemada claims that by carrying out his plan he will benefit the nation and society (*la colectividad*):

> Y esta gran operación que proyecto, ¿por qué ha de ser pecado? ¡Pecado que yo proponga al Gobierno la conversión de la *Deuda exterior* en *Deuda interior*! [...] ¡Demonio, si la conversión del *exterior* en *interior* es un gran bien para el país! Dígame usted, señor *San Pedro*, ¿qué va ganando Dios con que los cambios estén tan altos? Pues si yo consigo bajarlos y beneficio al país y a toda la humanidad, ¿en qué peco, santísimas biblias? . . . (*OC*, 1177)

Torquemada emphasizes the validity of his idea, challenging the priest's views and maintaining that the conversion of the debt will represent in fact, an act of charity – charity towards the State: 'Y dígame: hacer un bien al Estado, ¿no es también caridad? ¿Qué es el Estado más que un prójimo grande?' (*OC*, 1177).[34] Through this humorous image Galdós pokes fun at utilitarian ideas – propounded by contemporary voices and expounded in the novel by Donoso – about the individual need to act in the name of the community, that is, to the benefit of social progress and national wealth. The capitalist's identification of self-interest with the interests of society is exposed once more.

Torquemada's speech, which has been fittingly described as 'a fairly crude but by no means falsified version of the commonplaces of bourgeois capitalist doctrine',[35] constitutes a eulogy of pragmatism, rationalism and materialism. In keeping with the spirit of the times, Torquemada promotes an active and pragmatic attitude as conducive to material advancement. He urges his audience: 'Seamos prácticos, señores' (*OC*, 1100), proclaiming himself champion of technological and scientific progress, as his sponsoring of the locomotive demonstrates:

> Si yo no idolatrara la ciencia y la industria como las idolatro, si no
> fuera mi *bello ideal* el progreso, yo no patrocinaría la locomotora
> [. . .] [Y]o soy hijo de mi siglo, del siglo eminentemente práctico.
> [. . .] Adelante con la ciencia, adelante con la industria. (*OC*, 1101)

Torquemada's staunch views in defence of material progress here are not dissimilar from those expressed, in the novel *Nazarín* (written one year after *Torquemada en el purgatorio*), by the mayor of the village where Nazarín is finally arrested. Galdós criticizes both characters because of their brazen materialism, which is completely devoid of spirituality. The mayor believes that Nazarín, who attempts to put Christ's doctrine into practice, thereby disregarding progress and the work ethic, cannot be sane. Mysticism, in the mayor's view, does not contribute to the development of science, but only to economic stagnation and poverty. As he declares to Nazarín:

> ¿Y cómo he de creer yo que un hombre de sentido, en nuestros
> tiempos prácticos, esencialmente prácticos, o si se quiere de tanta
> ilustración, puede tomar en serio eso de enseñar con el ejemplo
> todo lo que dice la doctrina? [. . .] El fin del hombre es vivir. No se
> vive sin comer. No se come sin trabajar. Y en este siglo ilustrado, ¿a
> qué tiene que mirar el hombre? A la industria, a la agricultura, a la
> administración, al comercio. [. . .] [Q]ue haya la mar de
> fábricas . . ., vías de comunicación . . ., casinos para obreros . . .,
> barrios obreros . . . , ilustración, escuelas, beneficencia pública y
> particular . . . ¿Y dónde me deja usted la higiene, la urbanización y
> otras grandes conquistas? Pues nada de eso tendrá usted con el
> misticismo, que es lo que usted practica; no tendrá más que
> hambre, miseria pública y particular . . .[36]

Here, the reader is enticed to disagree with the mayor's defence of pragmatism and his rejection of spiritual values, as he is presented by Galdós as rude, cynical and ignorant (Galdós makes him use the incorrect form *haiga* in order to highlight and mock his false erudition (163). This is reminiscent of Torquemada, whose linguistic deficiencies are often used by the author to ridicule him).[37] It is significant that in the sequel to *Nazarín*,

Halma (1895), the administrator of the state of Pedralba, who expresses similar ideas to the mayor, is also portrayed in very unfavourable terms.[38] The administrator, like the mayor in *Nazarín*, is depicted as uncouth and ignorant (it is noteworthy that Galdós also draws attention here to the administrator's incorrect language).[39] It should not be assumed from this evidence that Galdós was against industrial progress. As I have argued elsewhere,[40] Galdós endorsed material, civilizing progress against traditional ideas, which regarded self-enforced poverty and the exaltation of mysticism as a virtue. In various articles written for the Buenos Aires newspaper *La Prensa* in the 1880s, Galdós campaigned for scientific and technological innovations, arguing against the traditional and widespread perception of poverty as a virtue and the consequent association of material progress with immorality.[41] Galdós expressed similar views in several articles written for this newspaper in the 1890s, where he continued to show a strong interest in industrial and scientific advances, attacking idleness and extolling the individual's capacity for hard work.[42] This is important in view of the tendency to assume that in his writings of the 1890s Galdós prioritized the spiritual over worldly concerns. My contention is that Galdós did not reject the kind of progress that led to improvement in social and economic conditions. What he condemned was excessive rationalism and pragmatism and hedonistic materialism, propounding a balance between the spiritual and the material. He conceived the spiritual not as the antithesis of the material but as the 'ethical' exploitation of the material. The author's criticism of Torquemada's – and for that matter Donoso's – utilitarian spirit needs to be seen within this context.

The Cost of Squandered Wealth and Idle Capital

Torquemada's obsession with preventing the waste of *material* resources is another manifestation of his utilitarian spirit. Torquemada's *credo* of thrift will suffer a great setback after his marriage into the Aguila family. From this point onwards, Torquemada's zeal for economizing is constantly contrasted with Cruz's extravagant and useless spending and her lavish and wasteful consumption. Unable to cope with the excess, Torquemada deplores the over-expenditure and waste generated by the refurbishment, decorative elaboration and running costs of the Gravelinas palace, and the luxurious lifestyle imposed by Cruz – including the hiring of a French chef, the purchase of an aristocratic title and her extravagant hospitality. Now, however, the author's criticism is directed more strongly towards Cruz's squandering than towards Torquemada's obsession with economizing against all odds. In spite of Torquemada's attempts to resist Cruz's wastefulness, he realizes from the very beginning that he is fighting a losing battle. Cruz completely dominates him, and Torquemada's lack of will before his powerful rival makes him a rather pitiful creature. As Hall has observed, Cruz uses Torquemada as an instrument: first as an instrument of the family's salvation from poverty and later, as an instrument of revenge on those family members who had humiliated her after the family had fallen on hard times.[43] The psychological torture to which Torquemada is subjected by his sister-in-law in *Torquemada en el purgatorio* is presented, in fact, as one of the factors leading to his illness and subsequent death in the last novel of the series (*OC*, 1117). Cruz's domineering and manipulative character and her victimization of Torquemada have the effect of inclining the reader's sympathies towards the miser's plight: for all his defects, Torquemada becomes a powerless victim in Cruz's hands. Any pity that the reader may feel for Torquemada is always tempered, however, by the humour and irony that surround this character.

Torquemada reacts bitterly against Cruz's profligacy and the new wasteful lifestyle he is forced to adopt. It is ironic that Torquemada, who is a leech on the poor and *produces* a *nonproductive* child, should attack others for being leeches – or being a drain – both on himself and on the nation. The *prestamista sanguijuela* thus refers to the builders, carpenters and others working in the renovation of his new home as 'sanguijuelas del rico' (*OC*, 1048). Also, he complains that his servants are leeches who are draining his wealth – a process he compares to the draining of the State's wealth – and calls them 'sanguijuelas del Estado' and 'dilapidadores de lo ajeno' (*OC*, 1115).[44] Appropriately, Torquemada, who thinks of his servants as useless and wasteful, vents his fury on an old servant who was, at the time, sweeping up rubbish and loading it into a wheelbarrow, hence associating him with waste (*OC*, 1115).[45] Later in the novel, the narrator notes once more Torquemada's anger at the waste represented by the superabundance of useless domestic servants, whom he compares with clerks in the State administration. He complains to Donoso that: 'su casa era un *fiel trasunto* de las oficinas del Estado, llenas de pasmarotes, que no van allí más que a holgazanear' (*OC*, 1125). Similarly, the numerous guests who attend the Aguilas' *tertulias* also represent, in Torquemada's view, a drain on his finances. This point is made in a passage in which Cruz's lavish entertaining is aptly described by Torquemada as a '*desagüe* sin término de sus líquidos' (*OC*, 1075 [my emphasis]), the use of the term 'líquidos' here adding vividness to the image of the money being drained away. What Torquemada cannot accept is that the guests are *taking* without *giving* anything in return. As he humorously puts it: '¿Qué beneficio líquido le aportaba aquella gente?' (*OC*,1076). Towards the end of the series, when he is approaching his death, Torquemada will be reluctant to leave his riches to the poor because he believes that the poor would simply drain his resources. In line with contemporary views, Torquemada assumes that any money that comes their way is wastefully spent. Thus, he will only agree to give his money away if he receives guarantees that his soul will be saved in exchange for his charity.

Torquemada's attempts to prevent material resources from being 'drained' are paralleled by his preoccupation with saving the costs associated with idle capital. There is an interesting episode in *Torquemada en el purgatorio* in which Torquemada associates work with utility and hygiene on the one hand, and idleness and leisure time with waste and lack of hygiene on the other. This echoes contemporary beliefs linking good hygiene (both physical and moral) with economic productivity and profit, and, it followed, disease with economic waste. In this episode, Torquemada's antagonism to lack of activity makes him resent a holiday that he is 'forced' to take with the Aguila family in Hernani, on the Basque coast, as he regards leisure time as idle, non-productive time. The narrator points out that Torquemada detests the countryside because he associates it with idleness and economic waste. In Hernani, not only is he forced into idleness, becoming non-productive, but is also made to *despilfarrar*. As the narrator comments:

> ¡Ay Dios mío, qué aburrimiento el de Torquemada en las Provincias, y qué destemplado humor gastaba, siempre [. . .] renegando de todo, encontrando malas las aguas, desabridos los

alimentos, cargantes las personas, horrible el cielo, dañino el aire! Su centro era Madrid: fuera de aquel Madrid en que había vivido los mejores años de su vida y ganado tanto dinero, no se encontraba el hombre [. . .] La nostalgia le consumía, y el verse imposibilitado de correr tras el fugaz ochavo, de dar órdenes a este y al otro agente. Aborrecía el descanso; su naturaleza exigía la preocupación continua del negocio [. . .] [A]bominaba de la sociedad ociosa que le rodeaba, tanto vago insustancial, tanta gente que no piensa más que en arruinarse. Para él, el colmo del despilfarro era dar dinero a fondistas y posaderos o a los gandules que agarran en el baño a las señoras para que no se ahoguen. (*OC*, 1057–8)

Torquemada links the city with hygiene because there he can be productive. Inversely, he associates the countryside with miasmas.[46] Thus, when Cruz, aware of Torquemada's misery, decides that the family should return to Madrid, the narrator writes, humorously:

¡Con qué alegría vio [Torquemada] el semblante risueño de su cara villa [. . .] Y ¡qué hermosura de calor picante! Que no le dijeran a él que había lugares en el mundo más higiénicos. Para miasmas, Hernani, que por ser cargante en todo, hasta tenía nombre de música. ¡Cuándo se ha visto, Señor, que los pueblos se llamen como las óperas? (*OC*, 1065)

It needs to be noted that the humorous image of an over-pragmatic Torquemada, obsessed with work and productivity, is offset in this episode by the narrator's clear allusions to the protagonist's misery at being taken out of his 'natural' city environment. Torquemada's unhappiness is such that it leads both Cruz and Rafael to reflect on their selfishness and feel intense pity for the man who has been abused and manipulated for the sake of the family's redemption (*OC*, 1063–4).

If Torquemada's association of hygiene with productivity conforms with ideas of the time, he does not endorse the contemporary vision of the countryside as healthy and hygienic. When the first Valentín falls ill, Doctor Quevedo – Torquemada's son-in-law – recommends as a solution 'ponerle un cencerro al pescuezo, soltarle en el campo en medio de un ganado y no traerle a Madrid hasta que esté bien bruto' (*OC*, 915). The beneficial hygienic influence of the countryside and fresh air, and the effects of city life on the population's physical, mental and moral health, were emphasized by hygienists during this period, who saw urban centres as a focus of physical and moral infection and diseases. The renowned public health expert, Philippe Hauser, for instance, commented on the physical and moral 'mefitismo' (foul smells) generated by human agglomerations in towns and cities, stressing the salubrious and invigorating influence of country life. Echoing anxieties about racial degeneration, Hauser also underlined the degenerative effects that the urban environment had on the city poor, which were often contrasted to the healthy lives of the rural poor.[47]

Torquemada's negative attitude towards the countryside can be explained by the fact that it had a complex symbolism during the eighteenth and nineteenth centuries. As Corbin has observed, the utopian vision of life in the countryside began to be undermined by a more realistic one, as filth and detritus began to mar its image. As ideas about urban public hygiene spread, towns were gradually being cleared of rubbish and dirt. The town became the place of the imputrescible, symbolized by money and wealth. The countryside, on the other hand, remained steeped in poverty and putrid excrement, which was believed to generate dangerous miasmas.[48] It could be said that Torquemada has a vision of the city as the place of money, the 'imputrescible', hence his dislike of the countryside. His sanctification of work leads the practical Torquemada to claim that country places should not exist and they should be replaced by cities. As he declares to Rafael:

> Mis vacaciones son el santo trabajo. No me divierte esta vida boba del campo, ni le encuentro chiste a la mar salada de San Sebastián [. . .] El verde para quien lo coma; y el campo *natural* es meramente una tontería. Yo digo que no debe haber campiñas, sino todo ciudades, todo calles y gente . . . El mar sea para las ballenas. ¡Mi Madrid de mi alma! . . . (*OC*, 1064)

In Torquemada's mind there is no place for the rural ideal: the countryside is dismissed in favour of the modern industrial city – the site of business, utility and efficiency.[49] Once again, the humorous tone of the above passage allows Galdós to ridicule Torquemada's exaggerated utilitarian ethic.

In *Torquemada en la hoguera*, Torquemada had already expressed his aversion to the countryside, in contrast with ideas voiced by Bailón and Quevedo regarding the positive effects of fresh air. When Quevedo suggests country life as a remedy for

Valentín's poor health (which he believes to be caused by excessive study), the narrator notes that in spite of Torquemada's willingness to follow his instructions for the sake of his son's health, he abhors the countryside and cannot see how any good can derive from it:

> Torquemada odiaba el campo, y no podía comprender que en él hubiese nada bueno. Pero hizo propósito, si el niño se curaba, de llevarle a una dehesa a que bebiera leche a pasto y respirase aires puros. Los aires puros, bien lo decía Bailón, eran cosa muy buena. ¡Ah! los malditos miasmas tenían la culpa de lo que estaba pasando. Tanta rabia sintió Don Franciso, que si coge un miasma en aquel momento lo parte por el eje. (*OC*, 915)

The humour at the end of this passage (the idea that miasmas are physical entities that one can 'cut in half') highlights Galdós's dismissal of the contemporary conception of miasmas as the cause of disease and, in particular, of the impact these ideas would have had on those who, like Torquemada, were largely ignorant and easily influenced by what they believed to be scientifically based and non-debatable evidence.

In the *Torquemada* novels – as in his other fictional and non-fictional works[50] – Galdós pokes fun at the contemporary obsession with hygiene through the presumptuous, foolish and ignorant Bailón. The narrator comments that both Bailón and Torquemada were concerned with public hygiene: 'La higiene pública les preocupaba a entrambos: el clérigo le echaba la culpa de todo a los miasmas, y formulaba unas teorías biológicas que eran lo que había que oír' (*OC*, 913). The reader is made aware, though, that the gullible Torquemada is dazzled by Bailón, whom he regards as an oracle 'en todas las cuestiones de un orden elevado' (*OC*, 913), as the narrator informs us. The narrator also alerts the reader to the 'necedades' that Bailón writes in his 'folletos babilónicos', commenting that the ex-priest 'era de los que con cuatro ideas y pocas más palabras se las componen para aparentar que saben lo que ignoran y deslumbrar a los ignorantes sin malicia' (*OC*, 913).

In *Torquemada en el purgatorio*, this zeal for hygiene is satirized in the episode when Cruz tells Torquemada that she plans to use two of the rooms in the Gravelinas palace (she intends to join them by bringing a partition wall down) as a billiard room, as she considers 'el billar' to be a 'pasatiempo grato, honestísimo, y muy higiénico' (*OC*, 1045).[51] To this, Torquemada replies, mockingly: '¡Higiénico el billar! ¡vaya una tontería! . . . ¿Y qué tiene que ver el billar con los miasmas?' (*OC*, 1045). Here, Galdós seems to be ridiculing both the contemporary obsession with hygienic matters, reflected in Cruz's statement, and Torquemada's pretensions concerning his desire to keep up with fashionable issues of interest. The narrator tells us that Torquemada's concern with hygiene derives from the fact that it was a popular issue at the time, and that in reality he did not have a sound knowledge of hygienic matters: 'Don Francisco, [. . .] en aquellos días, espigando en todas las esferas de ilustración, se encariñaba con la higiene y hablaba de ella sin ton ni son' (*OC*, 1045). Torquemada cannot regard billiards as hygienic because in his view it is a waste of time, as it is not productive. Idleness, leisure time and lack of hygiene are once more contrasted with work and (moral) hygiene.[52] Torquemada's obsession with work is reflected in his words to Cruz: 'Bien conoce usted que no sé ningún juego . . .; no sé *meramente* más que trabajar' (*OC*, 1045). Torquemada's over-enthusiastic work ethic becomes once more the target of Galdós's mockery.[53]

It is ironic that Torquemada, the man of action, should be afflicted with a stomach complaint (which manifests itself mostly in indigestions) that affects his business efficiency and prevents him from making money. This 'impotencia mercantil', as the narrator humorously puts it (*OC*, 1152), infuriates Torquemada, who regards the period of his illness as idle time, that is, as a waste of his potential to be economically productive. It is not a coincidence that Torquemada's stomach ailment affects his ability to digest food. The food that he cannot digest and ends up being vomited – or wasted away – is an apt metaphor for his wasted business and wasted chances to produce more money. A link is established in the text between Torquemada's personal finances and the national economy (to which his money and intelligence contribute) on the one hand, and his physical economy – the economy of his body – on the other.[54] His inability to work causes his capital to become stagnant and unproductive, making him unable to add to the nation's wealth. Furthermore, Torquemada's illness prevents him from carrying out his plan for converting the external debt (which is causing the economy to stagnate) into internal debt, a plan which he believes will be highly beneficial to the nation.[55]

In the same way as Torquemada's capital becomes stagnant, the food that he cannot digest accumulates in his body and congests his internal economy until it finally needs to be expelled. These images of stagnation and waste versus flow are related to contemporary beliefs, echoed in public health discourses, that air and fluids should be kept in a permanent state of movement, and to fears about lack of circulation or flow. These anxieties also found an expression in economic discourses, which stressed the importance of the circulation of money.[56] In *Torquemada y San Pedro*, the narrator notes how a sick and ill-humoured Torquemada witnesses his money stagnating, emphasizing his frustration and anger at the lost business that his ill health brings about:

> Tanto arreciaba el mal del marqués de San Eloy, que en todo abril no tuvo un día bueno, y hubo de apartarse absolutamente de los negocios, poniéndose más displicente a causa de la *holganza* y dándose a los demonios de sólo pensar que ya no ganaba dinero y que *sus capitales se estancarían improductivos*. (*OC*, 1162 [my emphasis])

Similarly, the food he eats goes constantly to waste because he is unable to digest it. The narrator highlights the parallel between wasted money and wasted food by juxtaposing the above passage with another in which Torquemada complains about the malfunctioning of his economy, that does not allow him to retain what he eats:

> Raro era el día que no devolvía los alimentos. [. . .] Comía con regular apetito, procurando contenerse dentro de la más estricta sobriedad, y a la hora, ¡zas!, mareos, angustias, bascas y . . . Francamente, era una broma pesada de la naturaleza o de la *economía* . . .
>
> —¡Ah! . . . —exclamaba palpándose el estómago y los costados—. No sé qué tiene esta condenada *economía*, que parece una casa de locos. No hay gobierno aquí dentro, y los órganos hacen lo que les da la real gana [. . .]. (*OC*, 1162–3 [my emphasis])

Torquemada's association of illness with idle, non-productive time is emphasized by the author in a passage in which the money-lender deeply regrets that 'lo ganado ayer con el trabajo se ha perdido hoy en la holganza' (*OC*, 1163), and he continues:

> Claro, van otros, y apandan los negocios, mientras yo me estoy aquí, quitándole motas al santísimo aburrimiento y mirando a mi

estómago y a mi economía [. . .] Es horrible vivir así, viendo que el
montón amasado con mi sudor se desmorona, y que lo que yo
pierdo otros lo ganan, se llevan la carne y no me dejan más que el
hueso . . . (*OC*, 1163–4)

The idea of waste is reinforced in the above quotation by Torquemada's comment that due to ill health he has been left with the
scraps. His obsession leads him to imagine that his inactivity not
only has caused his capital to become stagnant, but has actually
destroyed it, transforming it into a liquid mass that will eventually
evaporate:

otro síntoma de su mal [. . .] era la tenaz idea de que no pudiendo
trabajar, no sólo se estancaban sus capitales, sino que la inacción
los destruía, hasta llevarlos a la nada, cual si fueran una masa
líquida abandonada a la intemperie y a la evaporación. (*OC*, 1164)

The notion of wastefulness is pictured here through the image of
a liquid evaporating, the narrator's use of 'masa líquida' for
money being reminiscent of Torquemada's visualization of the
guests to the Aguilas' *tertulias* as a 'desagüe de sus líquidos', that
is, a drain on his capital (*OC*, 1075).

Torquemada's resentment at wasting the opportunity to continue to make money is highlighted again in the episode at the
Matías Vallejo tavern, when after informing his old friends of his
misfortunes, he protests: 'El [*sic*] escandaloso *en grado sumo* que
por los caprichitos de un hi de tal de estómago esté un individuo
desatendiendo sus intereses' (*OC*, 1173). Torquemada declares
his intention to continue to work in order to compensate for the
waste generated by his illness: 'He trabajado mucho, y pienso
trabajar más todavía, para reparar los quebrantos que esta jerin-
gada enfermedad me ha traído' (*OC*, 1169). In these two quota-
tions, the mixture of educated and vulgar language in the same
sentence introduces a humorous note that tempers Galdós's
criticism of Torquemada's compelling urge to avoid wastefulness.[57] Torquemada believes that his renewed appetite is a sign
that his health is improving and that consequently he will be able
to start making money again. Instead, as from this point in the
novel, his health takes a turn for the worst, as he will be unable to
recover from the disastrous effects of his eating and drinking
binge. By finishing the scene at the tavern with Torquemada
bringing up all the food and drink that he has ingested, Galdós
may be making an ironic remark on Torquemada's obsession with

preventing waste, the food which is vomited and wasted representing his squandered 'capitales'.[58] The irony is reinforced by the fact that Torquemada had previously thought that he ought not waste the opportunity of consuming the great variety of appetizing dishes offered to him.

As mentioned earlier, the root cause of Torquemada's digestive problems is shown to be the wasteful Cruz's tormenting of Torquemada. Further to this, the protagonist's stomach complaint could be interpreted as being the self-defeating consequence of his obsession with profit, which ironically leads him to waste his life. This second interpretation would contribute to Galdós's mockery of Torquemada's obsession with utility and profit. Also, the emphasis placed in the episode at Matías's tavern on wasted (vomited) food, represents a satire, on the part of the author, on ideological exhortations to recycle waste, something on which both the discourse on utility and that on public health insisted.

Wasted Lives: Torquemada's Utilitarian Approach to Death

Torquemada's attempts at preventing the squandering of material resources is paralleled by his preoccupation with preserving 'human' resources. In the series, Torquemada is faced with the deaths of two loved people: his son Valentín in the first novel of the series, and his young wife Fidela in the last. The humour that surrounds Torquemada's rational approach to death suggests the author's desire to ridicule the contemporary ethic of utility which Torquemada represents.

In *Torquemada en la hoguera,* the protagonist is confronted with the prospective death of his prodigy son Valentín, something he regards as a great loss to the nation. The death of Valentín represents, in Torquemada's eyes, a wasted opportunity, because his life could have been highly productive and profitable, not only for his father's sake – as Valentín would have been able to make money for him and add to his fortune – but for the nation's sake and also for humanity as a whole. His early death will prevent Valentín from contributing to scientific and economic progress. Thus, the pragmatic Torquemada is reduced to exclaiming that

Providence is not doing 'good' business by taking his child instead of 'less useful' lives:

> ¡Bonito negocio hacía la Providencia [. . .] Llevarse al niño aquél, lumbrera de la ciencia, y dejar acá todos los tontos! ¿Tenía esto sentido común? [. . .] Si Valentín se moría, ¿qué quedaba en el mundo? Oscuridad, ignorancia [. . .] ¡Vaya un ingeniero que sería Valentín si viviese! Como que había de hacer unos ferrocarriles que irían de aquí a Pekín en cinco minutos, y globos para navegar por los aires y barcos para andar por debajito del agua, y otras cosas nunca vistas ni siquiera soñadas. (*OC*, 919)

In *Torquemada en la hoguera*, Torquemada's inability to come to terms with what he regards as the illogicality of God's wishes is emphasized. In his utilitarian mind, Torquemada equates what is rational with what is just and useful, contrasting it with the irrational, unjust and wasteful. The association between rationality, usefulness and justice reflected the utilitarian tradition that human actions were ethically correct if they led to 'the greatest happiness of the greatest number', that is to say, if they produced the maximum social good for the maximum number of people.[59]

Valentín's life was wasted away before it could have been made productive. It becomes essential therefore that he is recycled. There are numerous references in *Torquemada en la cruz* and *Torquemada en el purgatorio* to Valentín's 'resurrection'. After his death he continues to appear in the novel as a spirit with whom Torquemada converses, until there is a point in which the spirit expresses a desire to be reborn. On one occasion, when Torquemada is in front of the altar where he worships his son, he thinks he hears Valentín saying to him: 'Papá, yo quiero resucitar' (*OC*, 967). The idea of Valentín being reborn haunts Torquemada thereafter. In fact, one of the reasons why Torquemada marries Fidela is that in this way he will be able to materialize his intense desire that Valentín be born again. In a humorous passage Torquemada says: 'Juraría que mi hijo quiere nacer y que me lo ha dicho . . . Pero yo, triste de mí, ¿cómo lo *nazgo*? . . .' (*OC*, 968). Here Galdós seems to be ridiculing Torquemada's wish to recycle his dead son. Later in the novel, when Torquemada believes to be close to realizing his desires, he insists that the child that Fidela expects must be a replica of the first Valentín ('el auténtico Valentín de antes en cuerpo y alma, con el propio despejo y la pinta mismísima de la otra vez'), because, as he says: 'Tiene que haber justicia, tiene que haber lógica, porque si no, no habría Ser Supremo, ni Cristo que lo fundó. El hijo mío vuelve [. . .] dado que deben pasar las cosas conforme a una ley de equidad' (*OC*, 1059). In this passage, the rational is once more set against the illogical and the unjust. Torquemada cannot comprehend the existence of a God who, by definition, should be fair but who does not comply with his pragmatic and rational views.[60]

The idea that God, or Providence, should make more just and rational choices is reiterated in *Torquemada y San Pedro*, when Torquemada faces the threat of Fidela's death. As he did when his son's life was in danger, Torquemada expresses his conviction that Fidela's life should be spared and that a 'less useful' life should be taken in place of hers. As he says to Gamborena: 'No sería justo ni equitativo que se nos muera tan pronto, habiendo por el mundo tantos y tantas que maldita la falta que hacen' (*OC*, 1140). A few pages later, Torquemada makes it explicit that it is the wasteful Cruz, and not Fidela, who should die, in a passage in which he perceives Fidela's death as 'una mala partida'. Here, the mixture of refined language and colloquialisms produce, once more, a comical effect:

> Verdaderamente era una cosa inicua, casi estaba por decir una mala partida . . ., vamos, una injusticia tremenda, que debiendo ser Cruz la condenada a fallecer, por razón de la edad y porque maldita la falta que hacía en el mundo, falleciese la otra, la bonísima y dulce Fidela. ¡Qué pifia, Dios! (*OC*, 1144).

The humour that surrounds Torquemada's over-rational perception of death continues in a scene where to Gamborena's advise that '[s]ólo Dios sabe quién debe morir [. . .] y cuanto El dispone, bien dispuesto está' (*OC*, 1140), Torquemada replies, 'amoscado':

> Sí; pero no es cosa de conformarse así, a lo *bóbilis bóbilis* [. . .]¡Pues no faltaba más! Admito que todos somos mortales; pero yo le pediría al *señor de Altísimo* un poco más de lógica y de consecuencia política, quiero decir, de consecuencia mortífera . . . Esto es claro. No se mueren los que deben morirse, y tienen siete vidas, como los gatos, los que harían un *señalado servicio* a toda la Humanidad tomando soleta para el otro mundo. (*OC*, 1140)

It is of interest that Torquemada states that God should be more *political* when choosing who should die. The use of the terms 'consecuencia política' and the humorous 'consecuencia mortífera' in the above passage is consistent with the contemporary concern with political economy. Torquemada regards Fidela's death, like the death of the first Valentín, as completely wasteful, and makes the point that God should be more discriminating, rather than taking lives arbitrarily: 'lo que ellos quieren [en el cielo] es llevar gente y más gente para arriba . . . No les importa quien sea' (*OC*, 1146).[61]

The issue of the illogicality of Fidela's death will be revisited once more after her death, when Torquemada tells Gamborena: 'en buena lógica, y sentando el principio de que tenía que morir una, ésta no debió ser Fidela, sino su hermana . . . Me parece que esto es claro como el agua' (*OC*, 1147). Torquemada's belief that Fidela's death is not logical or rational is highlighted in a humorous scene in which Gamborena urges him to accept God's will ('acatemos sus designios') and Torquemada retorts: 'Ataquemos . . ., digo, acatemos todo lo que usted quiera' (*OC*, 1147). Later, when receiving the visitors' condolences, he repeats the humorous pun, stressing once more the arbitrariness of God's wishes: 'Desgracia tremenda, inesperada . . . ¿Quién habría de esperar, si lo natural era que . . .? [. . .] [N]o hay consuelo, ni puede haberlo . . . *Ataquemos*, digo, acatemos los designios . . .' (*OC*, 1149).

From the point of view of contemporary ideas that emphasized the economic value of women and good motherhood in the generation of healthy and productive offspring and members of society,[62] one could read irony into the fact that Fidela not only gives birth to a cretin, but her death prevents her from producing more children. In this respect, it needs to be remembered that in *Torquemada en la cruz*, Donoso advised Torquemada that he should remarry in order to produce 'useful citizens' in the benefit of the material progress and prosperity of the nation. This allows Galdós to comment satirically on the ethic of utility – represented by Donoso – and, more specifically, on the contemporary perception of women as instruments for the improvement of the race. It needs to be noted that, unlike in the case of Valentín, Torquemada does not seem to regard Fidela's death as wasteful from an economic point of view. For him Fidela's death represents, rather, a waste of youth. The narrator comments on Torquemada's feelings moments before Fidela's death:

> El mismo terror que invadía su alma le sugirió ardiente anhelo de ver el tristísimo cuadro de aquella peciosa vida, próxima a

extinguirse en lo mejor de la edad, burla horrorosa de la lógica, del sentido común y aun de las leyes de la Naturaleza, *sacrosantas*, sí, señor, *sacrosantas* cuando no se dejan influir, ¡cuidado!, de las arbitrariedades que vienen de arriba'. (*OC*, 1143)

In Torquemada's eyes, the deaths of Valentín and Fidela are unjust and illogical, and from this perspective God is seen as 'squandering' the fruit of his creation.

It is ironic that Torquemada, who allows nothing to be wasted and is incapable of comprehending the idea of giving without receiving something in exchange, loses his son Valentín, a mathematical genius, to meningitis and fathers a second degenerate child, as we shall see in the next chapter. It is similarly ironic that Torquemada, deeply resentful about the 'idle' time and the wasted business opportunities that his illness means, should finally die without being able to carry out his debt conversion plan, a project fixed on his mind to the very moment of his death.

NOTES

1   Samuel Smiles, *Self-Help* (London: John Murray, 1958), p. 35.
2   Ibid., p. 36. Smiles once more stresses the importance of self-help for national growth when he writes: 'The spirit of self-help is the root of all genuine growth in the individual; and, exhibited in the lives of many, it constitutes the true source of national vigour and strength' (p. 35). It has been argued (Asa Briggs, '*Self-Help*: A Centenary Introduction', in Samuel Smiles, *Self-Help* [London: John Murray, 1958], p. 10) that the great success of *Self-Help* was partly due to its author's eloquent and forceful style, of which the above quotation is an obvious example.
3   Asa Briggs, *Victorian People: A Reassessment of Persons and Themes 1851–67* (Harmondsworth: Penguin, 1965), p. 132.
4   Ibid., p. 126.
5   Briggs, '*Self-Help*: A Centenary Introduction', p. 9. Smiles was to write other books in which he continued to promote the gospel of work and the values associated with it: *Character* (1871), *Thrift* (1875), and *Duty* (1880). It is noteworthy that all of these, like *Self-Help*, were translated into Spanish.
6   Ibid., p. 17. Briggs notes that in 1884 Grant Allen, a prolific rationalist author, wrote a book entitled *Biographies of Working Men*, in which he acknowledged his debt to Smiles.
7   It is well known that Galdós was a member of the Madrid Ateneo, like Rafael Labra and other Krausist figures.
8   Rafael María de Labra, 'El esfuerzo individual' (Discurso pronunciado en la inauguración del Curso Académico de 1878–9, del

Ateneo Mercantil de Madrid, octubre de 1878), in *Discursos políticos, académicos y forenses* (Primera Serie) (Madrid: Imprenta de Aurelio J. Alaria, 1884), pp. 203–16, 212–13.

9   Valentín Morán, 'Conferencias para obreros', *Revista de la Sociedad Económica Matritense*, 5 (1879), 28–31.

10   Smiles, *Self-Help*, pp. 58–9.

11   This point is made in Stanley Hollander, *The Economics of John Stuart Mill* (Oxford: Blackwell, 1985); and in Wyndham H. Burton, *James Mill on philosophy and education* (London: Athlone Press, 1973).

12   A Spanish version of *Character* appeared in 1892. See *El carácter*. Tr. by Emilio Soulère (Paris: Garnier Hermanos, 1892).

13   As the narrator tells us in two footnotes (*OC*, 1099).

14   Michael Nimetz (*Humor in Galdós* [New Haven and London: Yale University Press, 1968], pp. 170–1) has pointed out that Torquemada's speech ('a thorough recapitulation of everything Torquemada has assimilated in the way of refinement') constitutes Galdós's greatest triumph in the field of verbal comedy. Nimetz argues that Torquemada is fully aware of the vacuity of his speech, unlike those in the audience, who, impressed – and duped – by Torquemada's oratory, applaud him enthusiastically. Although Torquemada's honesty when disclaiming his oratorical success is debatable (see, in this respect, H. B. Hall, 'Torquemada: The man and his language', in J. E. Varey [ed.], *Galdós Studies* [London: Tamesis, 1970], pp. 136–63, 157–8) it cannot be denied that he manages to pass himself off as an eloquent and knowledgeable speaker. It is therefore the audience – members of Madrid's professional and business elite – which becomes the target of a harsher and more merciless attack by the author. As in other parts of the series, the protagonist is saved from receiving the full force of Galdós's sarcasm.

15   *In Torquemada en la cruz*, Torquemada had already been shown priding himself on being 'tan trabajador como el primero; y desde la más tierna infancia . . .' (*OC*, 946).

16   I agree with those critics like Robert Kirsner ('Pérez Galdós' vision of Spain in *Torquemada en la hoguera*', *Bulletin of Hispanic Studies*, 27 [1950], 229–35) who have seen the character of Torquemada as a figure that is comic and tragic at the same time. The over-rational Torquemada does not comprehend – not even before his death (as he dies unrepentant) – the meaning of the notions of charity, altruism and honesty, claiming that he has no sins and that he has not hurt or offended anyone. I believe that if there is here a mockery of a man who prides himself on being the complete opposite of what he really is, there is also a sense of pity which derives from Torquemada's lack of awareness of his own moral deficiencies.

17   See ch. 13 of *Self-Help*, in particular. In the prologue to the 1885 edition to *Self-Help*, Smiles made the point that success which had been achieved through dishonest means was infamous and worthless.

18   Tom Bell ('Evolutionary theory in the *novelas contemporáneas* of Benito Pérez Galdós' [unpublished Ph.D. thesis, University of Sheffield, 2003], p. 4) has noted that the term 'the survival of the fittest'

was coined by Herbert Spencer – who was greatly influential in Spain in the last third of the nineteenth century – and later broadly adopted by Darwin. Spencer's evolutionary perspective on socio-economic dynamics, Bell adds, provided scientific underpinning to *laissez-faire* economics, which made his work tremendously successful both in Europe and in the USA.

[19] Torquemada goes on to promote, rather crudely, the capitalist utilitarian ethic in a passage which, as Geraldine Scanlon has observed ('Torquemada: "Becerro de oro"' , *Modern Language Notes*, 91 [1976], 264–76, 271), represents a grotesque parody of the Sermon on the Mount: 'Busca y encontrarás, que dijo el otro. Sólo hay que sudar, moverse, aguzar la entendedera, *en una palabra*, trabajar, *ora* sea en éste, *ora* en el otro oficio. Pero lo que es dándose la gran vida en paseos y jaranas, charlando en los casinos o enredando con las buenas mozas *(Risas)*, no se gana el pan de cada día . . ., y el pan está allí, allí, vedlo, allí. Pero es menester que vayáis a cogerlo; porque él, el pan, no puede venir a buscarnos a nosotros. No tiene pies, se está muy quietecito esperando que vaya a cogerlo el hombre, a quien el Altísimo ha dado pies para correr tras el pan, inteligencia para saber dónde está, ojos para verlo y manos para agarrarlo . . .' (*OC*, 1100).

[20] Smiles, *Self-Help*, p. 115. Smiles insists on this idea when he states that: 'It was not by luck or accident that these [self-made] men have achieved distinction, but by sheer industry and hard work' (p. 169). The energy of will and courage of these heroes of self-help is constantly emphasized in his book.

[21] See nn.41, 42.

[22] I have made this point, for instance, in respect of *Fortunata y Jacinta* (1886–7), *Angel Guerra* (1890–1), *Nazarín* (1895), *Halma* (1895) and *Misericordia* (1897). See *Images of Filth: Deviancy and Control in the Novels of Galdós* (Liverpool: Liverpool University Press, 2003).

[23] Geraldine Scanlon, who has briefly analysed the notion of the self-help ethic in *Marianela* (1878) and *El doctor Centeno* (1883), has observed that, in spite of the rather idealistic and optimistic attitude shown by Galdós at the end of *Marianela* regarding ideas on self-help, the later novel *El doctor Centeno* is not the story of the successful self-made man that Galdós seemed to promise in the earlier *Marianela*. According to Scanlon, *El doctor Centeno* clearly exposes the inadequacy of the nineteenth-century belief that the poor could improve their status in life through hard work and thrift. Even in the more optimistic *Marianela*, Scanlon argues, self-help is not presented by Galdós as a panacea: good luck, and not just perseverance and initiative, are shown to play an important role in worldly success. See her *Pérez Galdós: Marianela* (Critical Guides to Spanish Texts) (London: Tamesis, 1988), pp. 53–6; and '*El doctor Centeno*: A study in obsolescent values', *Bulletin of Hispanic Studies*, LV, 3 (1978), 245–53. In the *Torquemada* series, no matter how hard working, thrifty and persevering Torquemada may be, it is made clear that the real reasons for his success are less savoury.

24   The undeserving poor were those whose impoverishment and their
     failure to succeed in life were seen as a function of their own (innate)
     weaknesses and propensity for 'vices', and who were therefore not
     worthy, or 'deserving', of assistance. As I have discussed elsewhere
     (*Visions of Filth: Deviancy and Social Control in the Novels of Galdós*
     [Liverpool: Liverpool University Press, 2003]), Galdós identifies a
     'deserving' and an 'undeserving' category of poor in his fictional
     works mentioned in n.22, where he draws attention to the difficulty
     of differentiating between both categories. This explains the author's
     ambiguous position in these fictional works towards begging and the
     related issue of the indiscriminate distribution of charity. As we shall
     see in Chapter 3, in the *Torquemada* series Galdós similarly problema-
     tizes the issue of charity-giving, although here, once more, he refuses
     to disclose his views on how charitable funds should be administered.
25   One commentator writing for this journal pointed out: 'Es indispen-
     sable ahorrar, porque la mejora individual y el progreso social son
     imposibles sin el capital, y el capital es imposible sin el ahorro': *La
     Voz de la Caridad* (15 December 1880), 251.
26   Smiles, *Self-Help*, p. 286. The practice of thrift was seen to be impor-
     tant for both individual and social well-being.
27   In a chapter of *Self-Help* entitled 'Money: its use and abuse', Smiles
     praised the thrifty, while condemning those who wasted their
     resources, claiming that the latter have never contributed to the
     progress of the nation. Smiles also commented on the improvident
     'man's' lack of self-dependence. As he stated: 'the man who is always
     hovering on the verge of want is in a state not far removed from that
     of slavery' (p. 285).
28   Ibid., p. 286. Smiles developed these ideas in a later book entitled
     Thrift (1875).
29   Ibid., p. 298. He commented that 'to hoard for mere wealth's sake is
     the characteristic of the narrow-souled and the miserly', warning
     against 'inordinate saving': *Self-Help*, p. 298. Smiles stressed that the
     root of evil is the love of money, not money itself, and criticized the
     businessman who only lives for himself, to the point that he only
     cares for other human beings 'in so far as they minister to his ends'
     (p. 298). Torquemada, full of avarice and selfishness, typifies the
     kind of businessman described by Smiles.
30   Later in the century, Hobson argued that workers in economically
     advanced nations did not have the spending power to maintain the
     expansion of capitalism. Hence, capitalists sought out new, global
     markets, benefiting from the infrastructure provided by imperial
     conquest. See J. A. Hobson, *Imperialism: A Study* (1902). Lenin,
     influenced by Hobson, made the same argument.
31   Tolosa Latour's observation on the circulation of money is relevant
     in this respect. As he points out, money is 'útil cuando circula como
     los glóbulos rojos, ponzoños[o] cuando se estanca, originando la
     avaricia, ese paludismo de las almas ruines'. See Manuel Tolosa
     Latour, 'Concepto y fines de la higiene popular', in *Discursos leídos en
     la Real Academia de Medicina para la recepción pública del académico electo*

Manuel de Tolosa Latour (Madrid: Est. Tip. de la viuda e hijos de Tello, 1900), pp. 7–43, 33.

[32] The idea that one should be useful to society was also stressed by Smiles. All of the self-made men described in *Self-Help* are said to contribute to the wealth and prosperity of their countries.

[33] Taking a different view, Bell (p. 147) has observed that from the perspective of the links between evolutionary theory and political economy, there is a connection between the 'sterility' of Torquemada's wealth and that of the San Eloy dynasty; and from this perspective, Torquemada's wealth does not benefit society. In contrast to other organisms, human beings are capable, through industrial innovation, of creating products which can further social progress and prosperity, hence counteracting Malthus' law. As Bell writes, Torquemada is neither an industrialist nor an innovator, and his money is essentially 'bubble' money gained through the stock market. His only venture, the building of a railway line to his home town, leads 'nowhere'. In fact, it is not even clear that the line is actually built. As Bell explains, many of these projects came to nothing. Thus, Torquemada's firm belief that he can benefit the whole of society strikes a deeply ironic note.

[34] Torquemada had already voiced the idea that his project would benefit humanity earlier in the novel, when he tells Miquis: 'hará usted un bien a la Humanidad dándome de alta. ¡Tengo un proyecto! ¡Ay, qué proyecto!' (*OC*, 1175). Soon afterwards he repeats the same idea to Cruz: 'arreglárselas entre todos para que yo esté bueno dentro de unos días, porque, sépalo usted, importa mucho para la familia y casi casi estoy por decir para la nación y para toda la Humanidad, si me apuran' (*OC*, 1176). Also, when after the viaticum his health undergoes an apparent improvement, he assumes that God is allowing him to live in order that he can undertake his project of converting the external debt into internal debt, a plan which in his view would benefit the whole of humanity, or, at the very least, the nation: 'el Señor, dígase lo que se quiera, me devuelve la vida a fin de que yo realice un proyecto tan beneficioso para la Humanidad, o, *sin ir tan lejos*, para nuestra querida España' (*OC*, 1187).

[35] Hall, p. 155.

[36] Benito Pérez Galdós, *Nazarín* (Madrid: Alianza, 1984), pp. 162–3.

[37] This does not imply that the reader's sympathies are drawn towards Nazarín, whose views, particularly his self-enforced poverty and contempt for material progress, cannot be trusted due to the ambiguities which surround this character.

[38] His materialistic approach is reflected in his words to the priest don Remigio: 'Si yo no siembro, nada cogeré, por más que me pase el día y la noche engarzando rosarios y potras. [T]odo eso del misticismo eclesiástico y de la santísima fe católica es cosa muy buena, pero hace falta trigo para vivir' (*OC*, 4th edn, vol. V, ed. by Federico Carlos Sainz de Robles [Madrid: Aguilar, 1965], 1858). So the advice that he gives Halma is: 'pues yo que la señora me dejaría de capillas y panteones y de toda esa monserga de poner aquí al modo de un

convento para observantes *circunspetos* y *mendicativos*' (1844). The administrator's plan is to cultivate the land and to make a profit out of it, because, as he says: '¿De qué sirve lo *espertual* sin lo otro?' (1844).

39   Although a parallel could be drawn between these two characters (the mayor in *Nazarín* and the administrator in *Halma*) and Torquemada's narrow materialism, in Torquemada's case the humour detracts from a portrayal of this character in a totally unfavourable light. Galdós's criticism of the mayor and the administrator is unquestionably much more acerbic.

40   Teresa Fuentes Peris, *Visions of Filth: Deviancy and Social Control in the Novels of Galdós* (Liverpool: Liverpool University Press, 2003), pp. 140–2 in particular.

41   See, for instance, the article written for this newspaper on 14 April 1887, in Alberto Ghiraldo (ed.), *Política española*, I, vol. 3 of his *Obras inéditas de Benito Pérez Galdós* (Madrid: Renacimiento, 1923), pp. 299–310. Galdós argued that this centuries-old cult of poverty, which he referred to as 'espiritualismo malsano', still lying at the heart of Spanish culture, had thwarted Spain's economic progress and had been at the root of her poor performance relative to her more advanced European neighbours. In this article, Galdós propounds the Protestant ethic of work, which had an important impact on Catholicism after the emergence of industrial capitalism. He attacks Spain's traditional hostility to work, a heritage of primitive Christian ideas which associated work and material progress with immoral and sinful behaviour: see W. H. Shoemaker (ed.), *Las cartas desconocidas de Galdós en "La Prensa" de Buenos Aires* (Madrid: Cultura Hispánica, 1973), pp. 148–9.

42   See, for example, *La Prensa* (18 October 1890), in Shoemaker, *Las cartas*, pp. 408–15; *La Prensa* (11 January 1891), in *Las cartas*, pp. 435–7, where Galdós applauds the advances in hygiene and medicine; and *La Prensa* (15 June 1890), in *Las cartas*, pp. 395–401.

43   Hall, p. 154.

44   As Urey has noted ('Identities and differences in the *Torquemada* novels of Galdós', in Jo Labanyi, *Galdós* [London, Longman, 1993], pp. 181–98, 184. Reprinted from *Hispanic Review*, 53 [1985]), now that Torquemada incarnates both wealth and social standing – through his property, speech and titles – his position becomes synonymous with the State itself: the wealth and class he personifies is that of the State.

45   It is worth noting that, in one particular scene, the servants in the Gravelinas palace are shown eating leftovers ('pan y unas miserias de lengua trufada' [*OC*, 1113–14]). They are associated with the recycling of waste rather than with waste itself. In the same way as tía Roma in the first novel of the series, they are scavengers and as such, they can be seen as 'productive' – as they contribute to the circulation both of rubbish and goods – rather than wasteful (see, in this respect, n.22 in the Introduction). Interestingly, in *Torquemada en la hoguera*, Torquemada himself is seen scavenging on leftovers that the

scavenger tía Roma brings home (see my Introduction). In the mentality of the period, Torquemada, the leech draining the resources of the poor, would have been 'productive' on another count. As Labanyi has pertinently observed, money-lenders could be seen as necessary to the health of the economic system in the sense that they facilitate the circulation of capital, in the same way as leeches are used to drain excess blood in order to normalize the circulatory system: see Jo Labanyi, *Gender and Modernization in the Spanish Realist Novel* (Oxford: Oxford University Press, 2000) pp. 118–19.

46   In the late nineteenth century, embryonic ideas on the germ theory of disease diffusion ran alongside older miasmatic theory, according to which epidemic, endemic and other diseases were caused by polluting 'effluvia' or 'miasma' emanating from decomposing animal and vegetable substances, from stagnant water, from damp and filth and from close and overcrowded dwellings. The issue of miasmas and their pernicious effects was often discussed by Spanish public health experts of the period. Juan Giné y Partagás, for instance, devoted a whole chapter of his book to it: see his *Curso elemental de higiene privada y pública*, 4 vols (Barcelona: Imprenta de Narciso Ramírez y Cñía, 1872), vol. 1, pp. 47–59.

47   Philippe Hauser, 'El siglo XIX considerado bajo el punto de vista médico-social', *Revista de España*, 101 (1884), 202–24 and 333–58, 349. Similarly, a contributor to *La Voz de la Caridad* highlighted the noxious effects of overcrowded living conditions in cities, again revealing anxieties about racial degeneration. As he wrote: 'La mayor parte de las guardillas de Madrid constituyen un verdadero foco de infección y [. . .] a consecuencia de la atmósfera mefítica que en ellas se respira, es frecuente el ver esas caras macilentas y pálidas de los pobres que en ellas se albergan, esos niños raquíticos, entecos y escrofulosos, *verdadera degeneración de la especie humana*, plantel de enfermedades crónicas y de vicios diatésicos. ¡Ah! En Madrid no podemos admirar la robustez y salud que parece conceder la Providencia a los hijos de los pobres que habitan en los pueblos y aldeas . . .' (my emphasis): see issue 1 December 1875, 282.

48   Alain Corbin, *The Foul and the Fragrant: Odor and the French Social Imagination* (Leamington Spa: Berg Publishers, 1986), pp. 154–6. It is noteworthy that Galdós subverts the association of the countryside with health in novels written during this time. In *Angel Guerra* (1890–1) (2 vols [Madrid: Alianza, 1986], vol 2, p. 508) the priest Virones contests the image of the countryside as rural idyll by linking it with detritus and economic misery. Also, in *Nazarín*, the countryside is associated with destitution and infection, and often with ignorance and brutish behaviour. In *Torquemada en el purgatorio*, the author's position is unclear, as the reader is not meant to agree either with the utilitarian Torquemada or with the shallow Bailón, who, as we have seen, expresses a different view.

49   Torquemada's dismissal of the countryside in favour of the city is reminiscent of his disdain for poetry and his championing of science,

which is also consistent with his utilitarian and pragmatic ethic. As Rafael declares to some of his *tertulia* friends in a scornful tone: 'El [Torquemada] divide a los seres humanos en dos grandes castas o familias: poetas y científicos [. . .] Pretende que puede y debe haber ciertas . . . [. . .] reglas, procedimientos, algo así . . ., para que los hijos que tenga un hombre *salgan* científicos y en ningún caso poetas' (*OC*, 1039).

50   In a letter of 1893 to *La Prensa*, Galdós ridicules the exaggerated concern with hygiene when he speaks humorously of 'el aforismo novísimo que simplifica extraordinariamente la ciencia hipocrática: *Todo es mentira. Sólo es verdad la higiene*': *La Prensa* (17 July 1893), in Shoemaker, *Las cartas*, p. 480. Nearly thirty years earlier, in an article to *La Nación*, Galdós had attacked, in a highly sarcastic tone, the hygienic measures recommended against the cholera epidemic, such as to avoid 'las impresiones fuertes': see issue of 15 October 1865, in W. H. Shoemaker (ed.), *Los artículos de Galdós en 'La Nación'* (Madrid: Insula, 1972), pp. 140–1. This zeal for hygiene is also mocked by Galdós in his fiction. In *Fortunata y Jacinta* (1886–7), for instance, the narrator notes that one of the traders in the market advertises his 'turrones' as 'turrones *higiénicos*', as a way of attracting customers (2 vols, ed. by Francisco Caudet [Madrid: Cátedra, 1983], vol. 1, p. 395; [my emphasis]).

51   It is worth noting, in this regard, that in the late nineteenth century in Britain, billiards was viewed as a respectable pastime that could be legitimately offered by public libraries as a means of counter-attracting workers from 'irrational' recreation: see Robert Snape, 'Betting, billiards and smoking: leisure in public libraries', *Leisure Studies*, 11 (1992), 187–99. In Spain, Concepción Arenal, among others, referred to the dangers of irrational leisure activities, which she regarded as encouraging dissolution among the working classes, advocating the creation of 'moral' and rational pastimes for workers: see *El pauperismo*, 2 vols (Madrid: Librería de Victoriano Suárez, 1897), vol. 1, pp. 281–326.

52   Samuel Smiles wrote, in this respect: 'steady application to work is the healthiest training for every individual': Briggs, *Victorian People*, p. 124.

53   It is interesting here that Torquemada and Cruz, two characters with completely different ethical standpoints, should allude to the same values and resort to the same discourses – in this case, the discourse on hygiene – in defence of opposing viewpoints and arguments. Characters in the series are shown to appropriate contemporary discourses, adapting them to their own specific needs, as we shall also see when discussing Gamborena's conceptualization of Torquemada as a 'savage within civilization'.

54   The use of the term *economía* and *economía humana* to refer to the body's economy was common in public health discourses of the period. See, for instance, Hauser, 'El siglo XIX', pp. 206, 210 and 216.

55   Thus, when during his illness he feels temporarily relieved of his

digestive complaints he asserts: 'la voluntad de Dios es ahora que yo viva. Lo siento en mi alma, en mi corazón, en toda mi *economía*, que me dice: "vivirás para que puedas realizar tu magno proyecto"' (*OC*, 1187).

56   As mentioned in the Introduction, these anxieties led to public health strategies to drain and recycle rubbish, in order to avoid the noxious accumulation of waste. In this respect, Labanyi (*Gender and Modernization*) has explored images of contamination, blockage and leakage (bad flow caused by over-accumulation) in a series of Spanish realist novels, drawing attention to the obsession, underlying the various contemporary discourses, with free flow (associated with the health of both the physical and social bodies) and congestion (associated with sickness). In her study she stresses the intersection between economic discourses (which insisted on the circulation of wealth), public health and town planning discourses (concerned with the recycling or 'circulation' of rubbish) and medical discourses (obsessed with the healthy circulation of fluids in the body). Labanyi observes how fears about the social body – that is, about the accumulated 'waste' and stockpiling characteristic of modern, capitalist urban life – were projected onto the female body, leading to the construction of women as sick, and to the perception of their bodies as pathological mechanisms beyond control.

57   Also, shortly after the relapse he suffers following this episode, he reiterates the inevitable waste caused by his sickness when he says to Cruz: 'si este condenado *fenómeno patológico* se agarra más, no sé adónde irá a parar la fortunita reunida con tanto trabajo' (*OC*, 1176). Here, once again, polished and colloquial language are used in the same breath.

58   The idea of waste is emphasized in this episode by the use of terms such as 'desembaular' and 'desembuchar', which refer to Torquemada's food being thrown up; and 'evacuar', which is used by Torquemada with the meaning of 'dispatch' or 'discharge' his business. It is ironic that Torquemada should use a term usually associated with the elimination of waste: 'evacuar' not only means 'to defecate' but it was also used in contemporary public health discourses with the meaning of draining waste from the streets. Torquemada's use of 'evacuar' in the sense of 'to dispatch one's business' (the narrator notes the protagonist's bitterness about his inability to 'evacuar' his 'asuntos' (*OC*, 1163)) may be related to the protagonist's visualization of his capital as being drained away.

59   For a succinct coverage of this, see entries on 'Utilitarianism' and 'The greatest happiness principle', in Ted Honderich (ed.), *The Oxford Companion to Philosophy*. 2nd edn (Oxford: Oxford University Press, 2005), pp. 352 and 936.

60   As mentioned earlier, Galdós's condemnation of an excessive materialistic and ultra-rationalistic outlook must not be taken to mean that he discarded science and modernity, and the social and economic advance these entailed.

61   The importance given by Torquemada to discriminating here is not

dissimilar from his ideas regarding the distribution of charity, expressed both in *Torquemada en la hoguera* and in *Torquemada y San Pedro*. Like many contemporary commentators on the issue, Torquemada believes in a rational and scientific – rather than indiscriminate, arbitrary and wasteful – distribution of alms among the poor, as we shall see in Chapter 3.

[62] See, for instance, Tolosa Latour, 'Concepto y fines de la higiene popular', pp. 32–4.

Chapter Two

Disease, Degeneration and Death: the Squandering of National Resources

Within the framework of the waste–profit dichotomy, one issue that permeates the novels of the series and constitutes the focus of this chapter is that of the degeneration of the race: the squandering of human and intellectual capital through degeneration and death and the effects that this had, or was perceived to have, on economic efficiency and social progress. Galdós's interest in rubbish and organic waste – as well as the recycling of it – is complemented and reinforced by his concern with the waste of human life through physical and mental disease and premature death. This reflects how the utilitarian discourse on waste contributed to, and intersected with, debates on public health and racial degeneration which emphasized productivity and economic gain. Although theories and anxieties about racial degeneration and the need to guarantee the future of the race came to the fore in Spain as a result of the 1898 crisis, their roots can be detected earlier in the century. There is enticing evidence in Galdós's work to suggest that he was concerned with the issues of racial degeneration and morbid heredity, and these issues certainly also inform the *Torquemada* novels.[1] This chapter will examine how the utilitarian ethic of the period was reflected in the writings of public health experts. It will also look at Galdós's stand vis-à-vis the discourse on public health and, more specifically, contemporary degeneracy doctrine. After analysing ideas on waste and inefficiency at national and social levels, the discussion will move on to explore, in the following chapter, the notion of personal profit and loss within the context of philanthropic activity as a commercial project.

Degeneration theory was first formulated in 1857 by the French psychiatrist Bénédict Morel. His work was continued and reformulated in France later in the century by the degeneration-ist psychiatrists Valentin Magnan and Paul Maurice Legrain, who had an impact in late nineteenth-century Spanish discourses on racial degeneration. Although the influence of an adverse social environment – the pressures and insalubrious conditions of urban life of the industrial period – was adduced as a major cause of racial degeneration, studies on degenerationism tended to over-emphasize the role of biological determinism, a link being established between degeneration and hereditary transmission.[2] Morel had established that the main factor contributing to the degeneration not only of individuals but also of the whole human species, was hereditary alcoholism. He proposed the theory that the children of alcoholic parents could inherit their alcoholism. Also, he introduced the concept of 'polymorphous heredity', according to which the hereditary transmission of a pathological condition could predispose the descendants to a whole range of different hereditary diseases, resulting from various morbid trans-formations. These would become aggravated as the hereditary progression continued, until the final exhaustion of the species.[3] The result was an accumulation of changing pathologies through-out several generations. The notion of 'polimorphous heredity' thus implied that the diseases suffered by the descendants did not necessarily have anything in common with those diseases from which they originated.

In Spain, the idea that the effects of alcoholism were transmit-ted and intensified from generation to generation, until the family line became extinct, was disseminated by Rafael Cervera y Barat, among others. In *Alcoholismo y civilización* (1898), where he records the research carried out by Legrain, Cervera includes a description and classification of a series of physical and mental pathologies – all resulting from the alcoholism of an ancestor – and their progression throughout three different generations. Notably, Cervera documents cases of rickets,[4] tuberculosis, menin-gitis, epilepsy, mental weakness, imbecility, idiocy, hysteria, mad-ness, violence, criminality, prostitution, vagrancy and alcoholism.

Cervera's text reflects his fears and alarm regarding the pernicious effects of racial degeneration on intellectual and human capital – and, hence, on productivity and national growth. As he emphatically put it: 'el alcoholismo engendrando idiotas merma el *capital social de inteligencia* [. . .] [y] con la mortalidad precoz abre otra brecha no menos considerable al *capital humano*'.[5]

It is significant that many of the pathological conditions cited by Cervera y Barat are echoed by Galdós in the *Torquemada* series. The four novels of the series are populated with characters who display a plethora of examples of physical and mental diseases, which often lead to their deaths. The first Valentín is a mathematical genius[6] who dies from meningitis at an early age. Torquemada is seized by epileptic fits, and towards the end of the series falls victim to a serious stomach complaint, which will lead to his death. Fidela has an anaemic complexion and is described as extremely thin and sickly, dying at a young age. Torquemada and Fidela produce a megacefalic idiot, who is afflicted by rickets and stricken with convulsions. Finally, Rafael suffers from neurotic disorders and ends up committing suicide. There has been a tendency to interpret these numerous cases of degeneration, disease and death in the series as symbolic of the spiritual and moral decline of Spanish society, as a message of failure and emptiness in a world dominated by material concerns. I argue that one needs to go beyond this 'spiritual' interpretation of the novels and read them in the light of contemporary theories of racial degeneration.

Safeguarding Human Capital: the Hygienic Discourse on the Value of Life

The issue of racial degeneration and prevalent anxieties about hereditary degenerative diseases and high mortality rates need to be examined within the context of contemporary discourses on hygiene and public health. The discourse on public hygiene had a deep impact on Spanish society of the time, an impact that is also clearly manifested in the novels of the *Torquemada* series. This discourse overlapped with discourses on psychiatry, political economy, anthropology, sociology, social statistics and with general social and moral commentary; it abounded in ideas on waste and profit. Public health experts firmly believed that intervening to ensure the vigour of the race was a major duty, and the underlying theme of their texts was the fear that the decadence of the race would lead to a decrease in the number of productive individuals.[7] In contrast to the individual approach adopted by psychiatrists, in hygienic discourses degeneration was seen as a threat to the vigour of the species as a whole, which gave the problem of degeneration a social dimension.[8] In this way, hygienists assumed the responsibility of safeguarding society's physical, mental and moral health. Hauser, praising the social role of the International Congresses on Hygiene and Demography, which took place in the second half of the nineteenth century and at the beginning of the twentieth century,[9] asserted that their aim was: 'resolver los problemas más arduos que atañen al mejoramiento físico y moral de nuestra raza'.[10] As the title of the Congresses suggests, population growth as a factor of economic growth and national wealth was a main concern of the participating hygienists, and reflected their internalization of a duty to serve as guarantors of the future of the nation. In a paper given at the IX International Congress of Hygiene and Demography, for instance, its author emphasized the significant role played by public hygiene in national progress, highlighting, through the use of statistical tables, the higher mortality rates of Spain in comparison with other European countries, and drawing attention to the economic loss that this represented for the nation. He stated:

> Todas las naciones civilizadas se preocupan más o menos del asunto primordial de la humanidad, de la salud pública; pero principalmente en estos últimos tiempos en que la estadística ha puesto de manifiesto el número excesivo de defunciones, en que la higiene pública ha puesto en evidencia todo su valer, y la economía política ha inquirido la pérdida grande que sufren las naciones que pagan mayor tributo a la mortalidad, es cuando las naciones han manifestado mayor interés por lo que atañe a la salud de los pueblos.[11]

The aim of hygiene, medical experts argued, was to make the maximum profit at the minimum cost, the expenditure saved by lessening disease being constantly emphasized in their texts. These drew attention to the vital role of hygiene in preventing the waste of human life: the loss of capital through physical and mental disease, and death. Angel Fernández Caro, in a speech delivered in 1886 at the Sociedad Española de Higiene, of which he was a member, alerted his audience to the economic repercussions of 'el *desperdicio* de la vida humana', highlighlting 'el *valor* de la vida' (my emphasis).[12] As he wrote: 'Hablar de la importancia de la Higiene es determinar el valor de la salud, es precisar el valor de la vida'.[13] Fernández Caro associates hygiene and health with productivity, profit, national wealth and social advance when he writes: 'todo lo que contribuye al bien social, todo lo que aumenta la producción y la riqueza, todo lo que fomenta las artes y la industria, todo lo que significa civilización y cultura, es higiene'.[14] Along the same lines, a commentator writing for the renowned medical journal *El Siglo Médico*, in an article significantly entitled 'La salud nacional es la riqueza nacional', asserted that: 'las naciones no pueden tener riqueza si no gozan de buena salud, y por ende [. . .] no pueden prescindir en manera alguna de la Higiene'.[15]

One aspect in connection with the loss of human capital often raised by contemporary hygienists and mirrored in the *Torquemada* series is the economic – and, hence, racial and demographic – value attached to childhood, and therefore, the economic waste represented by child diseases and mortality, whose cause was often attributed to the hereditary transmission of physical and mental discapacities. As it has been noted,[16] the pre-modern conception of childhood, according to which innocence and death went hand in hand, and a continuation of a high death rate among children was seen as inevitable, gave way at the end of the nineteenth century and beginning of the twentieth to a perception of child disease and death as something that could be and, indeed, needed to be prevented. Hygienists continually compared the large economic loss that child mortality represented for the nation to the relatively small economic cost of implementing preventative measures.[17] Although the perception of childhood as a *valor en alza* took on greater political and social significance at the beginning of the twentieth century in Spain, as well as elsewhere in Europe, the process began in the last decades of the nineteenth century, when the attention of hygienists, economists and statisticians was drawn to the issue. Fernández Caro, quoting another contemporary hygienist, remarked that:

> Un niño que muere antes de ser *útil* [. . .] no es solamente un motivo de aflicción para la familia, sino una *pérdida* real. Considerado desde el punto de vista del acrecentamiento de una

nación, la mortalidad excesiva de la infancia es una causa permanente de empobrecimiento. El que llegara a combatirla, al propio tiempo que evitaría raudales de lágrimas, añadiría millones a la riqueza nacional de su país.[18] (My emphasis)

One cannot avoid thinking here about the death through meningitis of the genius Valentín, for whom his father augured a brilliant future. As seen in Chapter 1, for the utilitarian Torquemada, Valentín's death represents a waste of intellectual capital and productive capacity. Torquemada makes this point when he comments on the 'bad deal' that Providence would make by taking such a *useful* life from this world (*OC*, 919).

The issue of child disease and mortality and the need to promote child hygiene figured prominently in the writings of those hygienists who took part in the International Congresses of Hygiene and Demography. The *Actas* of the famous IX Congreso Internacional de Higiene y Demografía (Madrid, 1898, 14 volumes) contain a series of articles on morbid heredity and child degenerative diseases, as well as child mortality.[19] The need to increase birth rates – which in turn implied a growth in marriage rates – and decrease mortality rates was stressed by hygienists taking part in the Congreso. Pedro García Faria, for instance, observed that:

> Dependiendo principalmente la vitalidad de una nación del aumento del número de nacimientos y de la disminución de la cifra de las defunciones, hay que procurar por todos los medios disponibles [. . .] el crecimiento de la natalidad y consiguientemente el aumento del número de matrimonios; por otra parte, deben suprimirse todas las causas evitables de enfermedad y de muerte.[20]

Over a decade earlier Fernández Caro had also propounded the idea that marriage was necessary for social progress, going to the extent of portraying celibacy as a social evil. He warned: 'El hombre necesita reproducirse, crear una familia; el celibato es un mal para la sociedad y para el individuo'.[21]

In *Torquemada en la cruz*, Donoso's proposition to Torquemada that he should remarry and have offspring needs to be read within the context of these ideas. To Donoso's suggestion, Torquemada replies, humorously: 'adónde voy yo ahora con una mujer colgada del brazo, ni qué tengo yo que pintar en el matrimonio, encontrándome, como me encuentro, muy a mis anchas en el *elemento* soltero' (*OC*, 965). Donoso firmly believes that Torquemada should marry in the interests of society, and that he is acting selfishly by opting to remain single. Thus, he rebukes Torquemada: 'Buena andaría la sociedad si todos pensaran como usted y procedieran con ese egoísmo furibundo' (*OC*, 965–6). In Donoso's opinion, Torquemada's celibacy, and hence his failure to produce offspring, is economically wasteful. The idea of producing children for the sake of economic growth and social progress is inspired by the notion, ingrained in contemporary thought, that one must return to society the benefits received from it, an idea which is in keeping with the give-and-take spirit of the period. As Donoso believes:

> nos debemos a la sociedad, a la civilización, al Estado. Crea usted que no se puede pertenecer a las clases directoras sin tener hijos que educar, ciudadanos *útiles* que ofrecer a esa misma colectividad que nos lleva en sus filas, porque los hijos son la moneda con que se paga a la nación los beneficios que de ella recibimos . . . (*OC*, 966 [my emphasis])

Donoso reinforces this idea when he explains to Torquemada that: 'La sociedad tiene también sus derechos, a los cuales es locura querer oponer el gusto individual. [. . .] Hay que mirar por el conjunto' (*OC*, 965). The notion that one should act for the sake of collective, rather than individual, interests was widespread among contemporary hygienists. Fernandez Caro, for instance, stated that, in the same way that society was responsible for the health and life of its individual members, '[e]l hombre, al constituirse en sociedad, abdica una parte de sus derechos en aras de la conveniencia general'.[22] Torquemada does not seem to understand, at this point in the series, the idea of acting for the good of the collective, as proposed by Donoso.[23] Galdós shows this in a humorous passage in which Torquemada thinks to himself: 'Pero ¡qué cosas tiene don José! . . . Salir ahora con la peripecia de que debo casarme . . . ¡Y todo por la . . . *colectividad!*' (*OC*, 966). The narrator's comment a few lines later (after noting that Torquemada had moved to a more spacious house) adds to the humour: 'Había él [Torquemada] oído mil veces *el casado, casa quiere;* pero nunca oyó que por el simple hecho de tener casa debiera un cristiano casarse' (*OC*, 966). Galdós seems to be poking fun here at Donoso, and through him, at the society he represents, a society dominated by ideas on efficiency and utility.

Valentín II: a Wasted and Wasteful Life

It is deeply ironic that, after Torquemada is persuaded of his
social duty to bring useful citizens into the world in the interest of
social progress and national wealth, he should produce a cretin,
hence contributing to social decadence rather than progress. In
spite of Torquemada's claim after Valentín's birth in *Torquemada
en el purgatorio* that his son is 'robusto como un toro' (*OC*, 1079),[24]
this is soon discredited by the child's rachitic complexion, a
symptom often linked to idiocy. The first reference to Valentín's
idiocy is made by Quevedo. In a conversation with Cruz, he
discloses his thoughts about Torquemada's son to her:

> El chico es un fenómeno. ¿Ha reparado usted el tamaño de la
> cabeza, y aquellas orejas que le cuelgan como las de una liebre?
> Pues no han adquirido las piernas su conformación natural, y si
> vive, que yo lo dudo, será patizambo. Me equivocaré mucho, si no
> tenemos un marquesito de San Eloy perfectamente idiota. (*OC*,
> 1083)

Later in the novel, Rafael will refer to Valentín's condition as
'cretinismo' (*OC*, 1090), cretinism and idiocy being used almost
invariably by contemporaries.[25] The causes of cretinism were the
subject of considerable debate, and in the 1830s and 1840s
became the focus of various official medical investigations and
fictional representations.[26] In spite of the uncertainty surrounding the causes of the disease, a morbid heredity was never ruled
out as a main predisposing factor, in keeping with the medical
climate of the period which tended to exaggerate the role of
biology.[27] As Pick has observed, in Morel's *Treatise* (1857) the
cretin was described as the emblem of racial degeneration: 'The
cretin', Morel remarked, 'is a pre-eminently degenerate being'.[28]
For Morel, cretinism came to represent the broader social problem of racial degeneration; the cretin's body thus becoming the
degenerate's body.[29]

Degenerates were regarded by contemporaries as *desechos
humanos*: the waste products of nineteenth-century civilization, an
economic cost or liability in an increasingly materialist and profit-
orientated society. Not only did they not produce, but they also
consumed, hence adding to national and social 'waste'.[30] They
were perceived as a drain on national resources, as they were

believed to represent unnecessary expenditure on hospitals, asylums and prisons, at least in terms of those degenerates belonging to the lower layers of the population. This is not Valentín's case, since, as a member of the wealthy classes, his family can make provision for him, as he is to inherit his father's fortune. Nevertheless, it could be argued that Valentín acts as a drain on his father's resources and hence, indirectly, on national resources by preventing the money from being invested usefully.

Indeed, Valentín is presented as wasteful from the very moment he is born, when he needs a number of specialists (humorously described by the narrator as 'eminencias' (*OC*, 1076)) to assist his birth. The narrator also tells us that Valentín needs 'dos soberbios animales de lactancia' (*OC*, 1081) to feed him, and highlights the large amount of money spent on his luxurious nursery and clothes (*OC*, 1082). There is one illustrative passage in *Torquemada en el purgatorio* where Fidela tells Rafael about Valentín's fondness for playing with his father's coins and with rolling them on the floor: '[Valentín] ha sacado la maña de meterle mano al bolsillo de su padre, y . . . No creas, empieza a sacar duros y pesetas y a tirarlos al suelo, riéndose de verlos rodar . . .' (*OC*, 1088). The symbolism of this does not escape Rafael: 'Simbolismo—dijo Rafael saliendo de su taciturnidad—. ¡Angel de Dios! Si persiste en esa maña, dentro de veinte años, ayúdame a sentir' (*OC*, 1088).

Valentín is portrayed as a leech, both on his father and on society: he over-consumes without producing anything in exchange. It is ironic that Torquemada, who is obsessed with waste, should decide before his death to change his will and leave all his money to his wasteful son, the only person that he feels he can trust. Torquemada even imagines that Valentín talks to him in his rudimentary language, uttering some words which he translates as: 'verás qué bien te lo guardo todo' (*OC*, 1191), something that is at odds with his proven wastefulness. Torquemada, however, believes that he is making the correct choice, as he seems certain that Valentín will grow up to be as economical with his money as he was:

> en la mayor edad, el hombrecito mío ha de ser todo lo que se quiera menos pródigo, pues de eso si que no tiene trazas. Ni tendrá afición al teatro ni a la poesía,[31] que es por donde se pierden los

hombres, y esconderá el dinero en una olla para que no lo vea ni Dios . . . (*OC,* 1191)

Even before the second Valentín is born, his father is tormented by the possibility that he may resemble the Aguilas and become a spendthrift like them. In a conversation in which he confides his anxieties to Fidela he declares:

> yo te aseguro que no quiero que mi hijo salga Aguila. Bien sé que Cruz beberá los vientos porque el niño sea como vosotras, como ella, gastadorcillo, pinturero y con muchos humos de aristócrata pródigo. Pero más quiero que no nazca si ha de nacer así. (*OC,* 1059)

When Cruz expresses the thought that Torquemada and Fidela's child will take after her and her family, Torquemada dismisses it squarely, with great indignation and rage:

> ¡Mi hijo ser Aguila! . . . —exclamó Torquemada fuera de sí—. ¡Mi hijo pensar como usted . . . , mi hijo desvalijándome! . . . ¡Oh! Señora, déjeme en paz, y no pronuncie tantas herejías, porque no sé . . . , soy capaz de . . . Que me deje le digo . . . Esto es demasiado . . . Me ciego, se me sube la sangre a la cabeza. (*OC,* 1056)

Torquemada, outraged at the thought that his son will be a spendthrift, exclaims, in a humorous passage in which the idea of waste is once more emphasised: 'Todavía no ha nacido y ya me le están *echando a perder!*' (*OC,* 1057 [my emphasis]). The irony, of course, is that Valentín's life is indeed wasted (*echada a perder*); also, Torquemada will be, in a sense, *desvalijado* by his son. The irony continues when we are told that Torquemada saw in the birth of the second Valentín a compensation for Cruz's squandering. As the narrator states: 'se aproximaba el gran acontecimiento, que esperaba el tacaño con ansia, creyendo ver en él la compensación de sus martirios por los despilfarros ociosos con que Cruz quería dorarle las rejas de su jaula' (*OC,* 1076). Following his give-and-take instinct, Torquemada claims to have won the right to be rewarded with a thrifty child:

> ¿Su hijo sería Torquemada, *como tenía derecho a esperar,* si el Supremo Hacedor se portaba como un caballero? "*Me inclino a creer* que sí—decía para su capote [. . .]. Aunque bien pudiera ser que la entremetida Naturaleza *tergiversase la cuestión* y la criatura me saliese con instintos de Aguila, en cuyo caso yo le diría al señor

Dios que me devolviese el dinero . . . , quiero decir, el dinero no
. . ., el, la . . . No hay expresión para esta idea [. . .]" (*OC*, 1076)

In his rational and utilitarian mind, Torquemada can only understand that things need to happen 'conforme a una ley de equidad' (*OC*, 1059). He is unable to comprehend a world governed by arbitrariness and illogicality. Hence his humorous idea that, in the event of Valentín turning out to be wasteful, God would be under an obligation to offer him some kind of compensation in return.

Not only is Valentín perceived as a human reject, but also as one that cannot be rehabilitated, or 'recycled', and made economically useful to society. The contemporary obsession with recycling organic waste was paralleled by the concern with the social restoration of those marginal groups – whether alcoholics, prostitutes, beggars, vagrants or the mentally ill – perceived as 'human waste'. The idea was that they could be reinstated into society and become useful citizens. Of relevance here are Morel's observations on the rehabilitation of cretins. In his 'Pathologie Mentale' (1846), Morel, following the research on cretins carried out in Switzerland by the influential Dr Guggenbühl, observed that there were two distinct kinds of cretinism: complete and incomplete. The former category was made up of 'those individuals in whom all that constitutes human nature from the point of view of perception, feeling, love, will, speech, action and caring for one's own life is altogether destroyed, to the point where man finds himself below the brute'.[32] Although it was believed that certain kinds of degeneration were open to improvement and some degenerates were restored to society,[33] complete cretinism was regarded as incurable. As Morel affirmed:

> I do not believe in the curability of cretinism when the illness is confirmed. All the pedagogic procedures, and best hygienic influences are in vain in the case of the complete cretin. He will remain what he is: a monstrous anomaly, a typical representation of the state of *dégénérescence*, which nothing could prevent.[34]

The portrayal of the second Valentín as an incurable cretin reinforces the idea of wastefulness surrounding this character and adds an extra dimension of irony to the author's attitude regarding contemporary views on, and anxieties about, population growth and national progress. In *Torquemada y San Pedro* it is made clear that there are no hopes for Valentín. The child's monstrosity becomes more accentuated as the novel progresses, particularly, after his mother's death, and those around him lose faith in the improvement of his condition. As the narrator notes:

Si [Torquemada] fijaba la atención en su hijo, se le caía el alma a los pies, viéndole cada día más bruto. Muerta Fidela, a quien el cariño materno daba un tacto exquisito para tratarle y despertar en él destellos de inteligencia, ya no había esperanzas de que la bestiecilla llegara a ser persona. Nadie sabía amansarle; nadie entendía aquel extraño y bárbaro idioma, más que de ángeles, de cachorros de fiera, o de las crías de hotentote. El demonio del chico, desde la primera hora de orfandad, pareció querer asentar sus derechos de salvaje independencia berreando ferozmente y arrastrándose por las alfombras. Parecía decir: "Ya no tengo interés ninguno en dejar de ser bestia, y ahora muerdo, y aullo, y pataleo todo lo que me da la gana." Fidela, al menos, tenía fe en que el hijo despertase a la razón. Pero, ¡ay!, ya nadie creía en Valentinico; se le abandonaba a las contingencias de la vida animal, y se admitía con resignación aquel contraste irónico entre su monstruosidad y la opulencia de su cuna. Ni Cruz, ni Gamborena, ni Donoso, ni la servidumbre, ni él tampoco, el desconsolado padre, abrigaban esperanza alguna de que el pobrecito cafre variase en su naturaleza física y moral. (*OC*, 1152)

The author is eager to show that Valentín becomes more animal-like as he grows up: 'cada día era más indócil, más bruto y más desposeído de todo gracejo infantil' (*OC*, 1161). His progressive deterioration is emphasized a few lines later, when the narrator observes: 'iba creciendo el heredero, y su cabeza parecía cada vez más grande, sus patas más torcidas, sus dientes más afilados, sus hábitos más groseros y su genio más áspero, avieso y cruel' (*OC*, 1161). The idea that Valentín could ever receive any kind of instruction is also dismissed (*OC*, 1161): there are no chances of rehabilitation for him. As the narrator comments, Torquemada sees in his son 'una esperanza absolutamente fallida' (*OC*, 1161). There is one scene in *Torquemada y San Pedro* where Torquemada attempts to revive the image of the genius Valentín, as he had done on previous occasions after his death, in a kind of blasphemous cult of adoration. However, on this occasion it is in vain: the memory of the first Valentín has now disappeared and, instead, it is the image of the primitive and wasteful Valentín that comes to his mind. The genius Valentín now says to his father: 'Ya no me acuerdo del talento que tuve. Ya no hay talento. Esto se acabó, y ahora, padrecito, ponme en una pesebrera de oro una buena ración de cebada y verás qué pronto me la como' (*OC*, 1152). This passage smacks of Galdós's mockery of Torquemada's attempts at recycling his dead son, the use of 'pesebrera de oro' highlighting both the animalistic and wasteful nature of the second Valentín. Valentín is linked with animality, brutality, savagery and lack of docility throughout. He is reluctant to walk on two legs, preferring to drag himself along the floor like an animal (he is described on several occasions as 'hocicando' on the floor). Valentín's language is described as a 'lengua monosilábica, salvaje, primitiva, de una sencillez feroz' and is said to resemble animal sounds. In *Torquemada y San Pedro*, his language is implicitly associated with the dialects spoken by the 'savages' Gamborena attempted to convert during his years as a missionary, and which the narrator describes as 'aullidos de cuadrúpedos' and 'cháchara de cotorras' (*OC*, 1122).[35] Valentín's animalistic instincts, destructive behaviour and violent tantrums contribute to his association with savagery (he is described as biting people, destroying toys and ornaments and torturing pets). Similarly, his liking for wine, as well as his thieving instincts, as noted by the narrator (*OC*, 1127, 1128), further stress his under-civilized nature.[36]

Valentín's primitive and animal-like appearance associates him with the pre-civilized, and reinforces his state of degeneration. He is an exemplification of the contemporary notion of the 'savage within civilization', a concept referring to the survival, within the civilized world, of sectors of the population which presented characteristics of the 'savage' and primitive peoples in non-European countries. Some elements in Western society, such as alcoholics, prostitutes, criminals, the mentally ill and the urban poor in general, were lumped together and identified, in contemporary anthropological and imperialist discourses, with the 'uncivilized' and morally and intellectually 'inferior' races of the colonies.[37] These 'morally diseased' sectors of society were presented as a threat to European races, in the sense that they were seen to constitute a degenerative process within the civilized world.[38] Degeneration was both 'inside' and 'outside'. The word *dégénérescence* was used in connection with both 'primitive' peoples in underdeveloped areas of the globe and 'alien' groups at home. As such, it became increasingly unclear whether degeneration was caused by civilization or by its absence.[39] This is reflective of the contradictory nature of degeneration theory, which posited degeneracy as a result of progress but, at the same time, lack of civilization. Further to his animality, stress is laid on Valentín's filthy state and his inclination to dirt. As the narrator writes:

> Mudábanle con frecuencia y siempre estaba sucio, de arrastrar su panza por el suelo [. . .]; las babas le caían en hilo sobre el pecho, y sus manos, lo único que tenía bonito, estaban siempre negras, cual si no conociera más entretenimiento que jugar con carbón. (*OC*, 1127)

Valentín's animality and filth are reminiscent of the portrayal of the 'cuarto estado' children in *Fortunata y Jacinta* during Guillermina's and Jacinta's visit to the slums of Madrid. The slum children, who are shown to have covered their face and hands in ink so as to look like blacks, are described by the narrator as 'una manada de salvajes' who 'no parecían pertenecer a la raza humana' (I, 324). When Jacinta first meets Pitusín he is also covered in ink (I, 329) and the character often appears in connection with savagery, rubbish and dirt. As I have explored elsewhere,[40] the concept of filth conjured up a variety of images in the late nineteenth century. The anxieties raised by the growth of social problems related to the explosion of poverty, such as mendicity, vagrancy, alcoholism, prostitution and the spectre of racial degeneration, found expression in the images of filth that appeared around them, images generated by the threat of social instability and disorder that these 'deviant' sectors of the population represented. Filth thus became a metaphor for disease, immorality, vice, disorder and deviant behaviour generally. In the *Torquemada* series, Galdós subverts this association, to an extent, by linking Valentín – a mixture of the working and the aristocratic classes, born and brought up in a wealthy environment – with filth and savagery and portraying him as a cretin. (It is worth noting, in this respect, the comment made by the narrator on the ironic contrast between Valentín's idiocy and the 'opulencia de su cuna' (*OC*, 1152).) Galdós's message here may be that, in spite of its association with the filth and immorality of the lower classes, degeneration – like other kinds of deviant behaviour – spread across classes, that is, it could affect anyone independently of their social station. Although certain degenerative diseases, notably, hysteria, anaemia and neurasthenia[41] were associated with the middle and upper classes (as we shall see, in the *Torquemada* series, Fidela is portrayed as anaemic, whereas Rafael presents symptoms of hysteria) degeneration tended to be linked to the lower layers of society, an association arising from the perception of these classes as threatening, and their behaviour as more difficult to control and contain.

Valentín's degenerate state, his 'monstrous' nature, has tended to be read at a symbolic level, often as representing Torquemada's moral monstrosity and, like the latter, as a manifestation of the spiritual and moral decline of Spanish society.[42] Also, Valentín's monstrosity has been interpreted as resulting from the inappropriate, destructive and 'monstrous' quality of his parents' union.[43] Sherzer, for instance, has seen in the second Valentín an inevitable product of the marriage between Torquemada and Fidela, an ominous marriage not only because of the faults in Torquemada's character (his selfishness and avarice), but also because of the anachronistic mentality of the aristocratic family with which he unites. Furthermore, in Sherzer's view, Fidela's decision to marry the usurer is unethical, and thus deserves to be punished. Sherzer has seen in these novels a 'punitive pattern of failure through loss of succession and death'.[44] The union between Valentín's parents is bound to be marked by death and emptiness, represented by Rafael's suicide – a direct result of their marriage, Valentín's abnormality, Fidela's death and Torquemada's own death.[45] Similarly, Weber has emphasized that *Torquemada y San Pedro* is fashioned around various examples of disease and/or the death of three major characters – Torquemada, Fidela, and their offspring, Valentín – who symbolize 'detrimental influences in Spanish society'.[46] Stressing the symbolic relevance of these cases of sickness and death, Weber argues that 'Galdós chose to represent the effects of spiritual and moral degeneration through the deaths of a passive aristocrat, Fidela, of a usurer turned aristocrat, Torquemada, and through the imbecility of their offspring, Valentín'.[47] Weber has come to this conclusion on the basis of three preliminary sketches of Torquemada, Fidela and Valentín which Galdós prepared in 1889, six years before writing the final version of *Torquemada y San Pedro*.[48] As he affirms, these three outlines – which bear many similarities with the novel, and which Galdós would have drawn up with a view to using them as a guide for the last novel of the series – are essentially medical case histories of these three characters. Although I agree with Weber that the focus of the sketches on these three characters as virtually medical case studies is revealing, it is my contention that one should leave aside Weber's and other critics' symbolic readings and look at these examples of abnormality, disease and death in the light of contemporary hygienic discourses on the future of the race, society and the nation.

A Family of Degenerates?

Within this context it is significant that not only Valentín but also both his parents, Torquemada and Fidela, suffer from afflictions (epilepsy and anaemia respectively) which at the time would have been linked to racial degeneration. This is particularly relevant from the point of view of contemporary medical thought, according to which, parents affected by some kind of physical and/or, in particular, mental degeneration would produce degenerate offspring, in whom the symptoms of degeneration would be more severe.

In medical books of the period, medical journals such as *El Siglo Médico*, as well as in the transactions of the various Congresses of Hygiene and Demography held in the last decades of the nineteenth century, there are numerous references to epilepsy and chloro-anaemia,[49] both as the symptoms and the result of a process of racial degeneration.[50] Like other morbid conditions transmittable via heredity, such as meningitis, tuberculosis, alcoholism, idiocy, rachitism, insanity and hysteria, epilepsy and chloro-anaemia were seen as links in a chain of degeneration, and hence also as a possible cause of more serious pathologies which could manifest themselves in future generations. It is not surprising, therefore, that a renowned public health expert like Juan Giné y Partagás would go to the extent of urging that '[la epilepsia] debiera [. . .] contarse entre los *impedientes* y *dirimentes* del matrimonio'.[51] The same attitude was adopted in respect of chlorosis, a disorder which became increasingly common during the nineteenth century and mostly affected young women.[52] 'Cloro-anemia' was regarded by Hauser as one of the 'enfermedades degenerativas' characteristic of the times.[53] The threat it was seen to represent led some medical men to state that chlorosis sufferers should be prevented from procreating. This is indicative of the anxieties generated by the production and reproduction of degenerates.[54]

Torquemada's epileptic fits take place after the deaths of Valentín I and Fidela. Weber has noted that in the preliminary sketches of *Torquemada y San Pedro* Torquemada's second attack (after Fidela's death) is not mentioned, and Galdós limits himself to quoting the portion of *Torquemada en la hoguera* dealing with Torquemada's epileptic seizure after Valentín dies. In the fully fledged version, Galdós adds that Torquemada had a similar fit when he finds out about Fidela's death, and simply refers back to the first attack rather than quoting it fully.[55] Galdós may have added this second epileptic fit in the definitive version of the novel in order to highlight Torquemada's proneness to epilepsy: perhaps Galdós thought it was a more efficient way of reinforcing the protagonist's predisposition to the disease than reminding the reader of his previous seizure in the first novel of the series. Torquemada has another spasmodic attack after his eating binge at Matías Vallejo's *bodegón* in *Torquemada y San Pedro*. As the narrator states: 'Gruñendo como un cerdo se retorcía con horrorosas convulsiones' (*OC*, 1172). The epileptic nature of this seizure would seem to be emphasized by the fact that he is shown to foam at the mouth on arrival at the Gravelinas palace (*OC*, 1174).[56]

Regarding Fidela's condition, it is noteworthy that when she falls seriously ill – an illness which will lead to her death – she is diagnosed as suffering from 'anemia y un poco de histerismo' by a doctor friend of Torquemada who shares Quevedo's opinion on the cause of Fidela's complaints (*OC*, 1138). Hysteria (which would explain Fidela's sensation of being suffocated by a ball in the throat (*OC*, 1138)) and anaemia, were both disorders categorized in the nineteenth century as 'female diseases'. This diagnosis by the two doctors, however, appears to be incorrect, as the more senior doctor, Augusto Miquis, is shown to rebuke Quevedo later for not having been fully aware of the seriousness of Fidela's symptoms. What Miquis does in fact find in the patient are the symptoms of 'depresión cardíaca' (*OC*, 1141). The narrator also alludes to Fidela having two attacks of 'dyspnoea' (an inability to breath) before Miquis arrives. The sensation of suffocation would thus be related to this rather than to hysteria. The fact that two doctors dismiss Fidela's symptoms as being mere manifestations of 'female diseases' reflects the contemporary (and often negative) association of women with nervous disorders.[57] Galdós may be criticizing here the over-emphasis placed by the medical profession on such an association, which could lead to the disregard of life-threatening conditions – as in Fidela's case. Furthermore, although Fidela is described as anaemic in the series, there is no clear indication that she suffers from hysteria. In fact, it is a male character, albeit a feminized one, Rafael, who is shown to display signs of hysteria, as we shall see.

Within the context of these ideas, for many of Galdós's contemporaries, Torquemada and Fidela's union would have been 'monstrous' in a sense that goes beyond the traditional interpretations offered by critics.[58] Fernández Caro, for instance, urged that it was necessary to avoid 'esas *uniones monstruosas*' (my emphasis) which transmit from generation to generation the hereditary predisposition to a pathological condition.[59] This is particularly relevant if we consider that epilepsy was believed to be generally transmitted by the father.[60] What emerges from this evidence is that in these novels there is an awareness on the part of the author of contemporary beliefs on, and anxieties about, 'inconvenient' marriages – unions between individuals who were predisposed to certain diseases – and the risks of a degenerate progeny that these marriages involved.

The issue of the control and regulation of marriages was often voiced by hygienists in the last decades of the nineteenth century and at the beginning of the twentieth century.[61] Tolosa Latour asserted in 1893 – the year of the publication of the second novel of the series:

> los padres son quienes muy principalmente legan estas enfermedades [degenerativas] a sus hijos, unas veces por haberlas recibido a su vez de sus antecesores, otras por haber provocado su futura germinación, desoyendo los grandes preceptos del Código científico, que rechaza toda *unión peligrosa* y estigmatiza los que dejan en pos de sí una raza decrépita, enferma o criminal.[62] (My emphasis)

Fifteen years later, in the IX Congress of Hygiene and Demography held in Madrid, Manuel Iglesias y Díaz referred to 'constituciones endebles' which are 'el fruto de padres débiles, bien por la edad avanzada, bien por los padecimientos de que se hallan afectados'.[63] Also at this Congress, Bernabé Malo stated that 'la herencia orgánica [. . .] representa [. . .] importantísima causa del vigor de la raza o de su degeneración; siendo por ello responsable en alto grado de la mortalidad infantil'.[64] In order to facilitate 'la humanitaria lucha contra la degeneración', Malo proposed the study of the state of health of the *cónyuges* and the discouraging or even banning of marriages in those cases in which a predisposition to hereditary diseases could be proved. This measure was to be complemented by the introduction of a book (*Libro clínico de familias*), which would include information on the family's clinical history and that of the previous two generations.[65] Ideas on the regulation of marriages had already been propounded by Galton, the proponent of the eugenic doctrine, in *Hereditary Talent and Character* (1865). Galton observed the decadence and degeneration of the English race, an issue that came to the fore particularly after the Crimean war. As degenerative traits were inevitably transmitted via heredity, the only possible solution was a strict control of marriages, that is, the prevention of marriages between 'inferior' people. For Galton, the control of the *quality* of the population was essential.[66] In his presidential address to the VII International Congress of Hygiene and Demography held in London in 1891, two years before the publication of the second novel of the series, Galton attempted to draw awareness to a number of questions in connection with the biological, intellectual and moral betterment of the race. In his speech, he addressed the problem of fertility (using, interestingly, the term 'productiveness' in the sense of 'fertility'), advocating the intervention of hygienists so that fertility could be placed at the service of the most 'deserving'.[67]

Notwithstanding the fact that both Torquemada and Fidela bear clear signs of degeneration, and despite the contemporary stress on biological determinism, Valentín is not presented as a product of congenital degeneration. Thus, although Galdós was fully aware of ideas circulating at the time on the issue of racial degeneration, he does not follow them unquestioningly, hence calling into question the validity of degeneration theory. It is significant that having all the necessary elements at hand the author opts for making no clear connection between Valentín's degenerative state – on which he focuses a great deal of attention – and a morbid inheritance. Even more significant is the fact that, in the preliminary sketches of *Torquemada y San Pedro* previously mentioned, Galdós had thought of a specific hereditary explanation for Valentín's condition, an explanation that was revealingly discarded by the author in the final version of the novel.[68] In these sketches, Valentín, as well as displaying the symptoms of idiocy that characterize him in the final version, is clearly described as an epileptic. In them, Galdós links, in an explicit way, the child's condition to his father's epileptic fits, as well as to his alcoholic state during the first days of the wedding – in keeping with the contemporary belief that drunkenness at the time of conception increased the chances of a pathological inheritance and the intensity of its ravages.[69] As Galdós wrote: 'en algunas ocasiones [Valentín] parecía un epiléptico – (antecedentes hereditarios: ataque del padre al morir su anterior hermano. ¿Engendrado durante la embriaguez de los primeros días de la boda? ...)'.

The description of Valentín's epilepsy in the sketches as a case of hereditary degeneration is consistent with contemporary degeneracy doctrine, according to which epilepsy could be inherited directly from a progenitor afflicted with the same disease. Also, epilepsy could be the result of an alcoholic inheritance, in compliance with the laws of polymorphous heredity, which stated that the alcoholism of an ancestor could become transformed and aggravated with each succeeding generation of offspring. In these preliminary outlines of the novel, Torquemada's alcoholism would explain, of course, not only Valentín's epilepsy but also his idiocy. Both epilepsy and idiocy (among other kinds of degeneration) were listed by contemporary hygienists as obvious examples of hereditary alcoholism. As early as 1876, the public health expert Juan Giné y Partagás referred to it as the cause of 'el idiotismo, la imbecilidad, la epilepsia y la predisposición a diferentes formas de la alienación mental'.[70] Later in the century, Cervera y Barat, influenced by French psychiatric discourse, observed that 'la herencia alcohólica es una causa poderosa de *degradación intelectual* en el individuo y la especie', stressing the idea of a progressive mental deterioration throughout the various generations of degenerates:

> A medida que se desciende de generación en generación en la raza de los alcohólicos, decrece también en la misma proporción la *resistencia cerebral*, hasta que se llega en este continuo descenso a la extinción total de las funciones mentales, con el *idiotismo*, o a la extinción de la familia, con la *muerte precoz*.[71]

Cervera noted that the 215 families serving as a basis for Legrain's study (and whose ancestors were alcoholics) produced, in the first generation, a number of 508 individuals, all of whom had been affected, whether intellectually or physically, by the alcoholism of a predecessor. According to this study, the main type of mental degeneration inherited from alcoholism was mental feebleness ('debilidad mental' or 'debilidad de la inteligencia'), a condition which embraced 'desde el hombre que llamamos simple u obtuso hasta el imbécil y el idiota'.[72] Cervera also drew attention to the overwhelming number of cases of epilepsy – 54 out of the 215 families – who were a direct result of the alcoholism of the first generation. He describes epilepsy as the result of 'la poca resistencia orgánica, la miseria fisiológica con que vienen a la vida los herederos del alcoholismo'; and continues to assert that: 'Esa miseria congénita hace que los hijos de los borrachos se desarrollen difícil y lentamente; son seres enclenques, enfermizos, y víctimas en gran parte de las enfermedades agudas de la infancia'.[73] Epilepsy is cited by Cervera, as one of those 'enfermedades de la infancia' to which he refers.

After having set up a neat pattern of associations in the sketches, Galdós will go on to subvert it in the fully fledged version of *Torquemada y San Pedro*. Here, not only is Valentín not described as an epileptic, but neither Torquemada's alcoholism nor his proneness to epilepsy are presented as the causes of Valentín's condition. Although in the final text Valentín is portrayed as having 'rabietas convulsivas', these seizures are not explicitly presented as the product of either his father's epilepsy or of his drinking.[74] There is no obvious indication, either, that Valentín's convulsions are a manifestation of epilepsy. Furthermore, in the final version, neither epilepsy nor alcoholism are clearly associated with Valentín's idiocy. Galdós was particularly intent on dismissing Torquemada's drunkenness and hence the link between his alcoholic state and his son's abnormality. He achieves this by making patently clear throughout the series that Torquemada is not an alcoholic. If anything, his temperance is emphasized. In *Torquemada en la cruz*, for instance, when in a visit that Torquemada pays to the Aguila family Cruz apologizes for not being able to offer Torquemada any wine, Torquemada declares that he does not drink wine 'más que los domingos y fiestas de guardar' (*OC*, 949).[75] Later in the novel, Torquemada boasts his sobriety and his 'pureza de costumbres' when he states, in an internal monologue: 'El, ni bebida; él, ni mujeres; él, ni juego; él, ni tan siquiera el inofensivo placer del tabaco' (*OC*,

971).` In the wedding episode (*Torquemada en la cruz*), when
Torquemada becomes deeply inebriated after drinking too much
champagne, his customary temperance is again reinforced by
Donoso's comment that: '[c]omo [Torquemada] no tiene cos-
tumbre de beber, le ha hecho daño el champaña' (*OC*, 1013–14).
Moreover, although Torquemada's drunkenness on his wedding
day is notorious, Galdós leaves no doubt about the fact that
Valentín was not conceived when Torquemada was under the
effects of alcohol. The author highlights Fidela's indisposition
during the day and, particularly, the night of the wedding, when
she develops a 'fiebre intensa' and is seen lying in bed 'en
profundo letargo febril' (*OC*, 1013); whereas Torquemada is
shown 'roncando desaforadamente' after his drinking binge (*OC*,
1014). Torquemada's sobriety is compounded by the author's
humorous remark that the reason why Torquemada gets drunk
on his wedding day is that he could not bear the idea of the
champagne *going to waste*:

> el novio creyó que no cumplía como bueno en día tan solemne si
> no empinaba ferozmente el codo; porque, lo que él decía:
> ¡Haberse corrido a un desusado gasto de champaña, para después
> hacer el pobrete melindroso! Bebiéralo o no, tenía que pagarlo.
> Pues a consumirlo, para que al menos se igualara el haber del
> estómago con el debe del bolsillo. Por esta razón puramente
> económica y de partida doble, más que por vicio de embriaguez,
> bebió copiosamente el tacaño, cuya sobriedad no se desmentía
> sino en casos rarísimos. (*OC*, 1012)

The idea that Torquemada is an alcoholic is once more effectively
discredited. Furthermore, in contrast to the sketches, in the
definitive version of the novel, Torquemada is not seen getting
drunk in the days that follow his wedding day, which contributes
to the author's dissociation of Valentín with hereditary alcoholism. Thus, in the *Torquemada* novels, Galdós can be said to be
distancing himself from his previous straightforward endorsement (in the sketches) of the hereditary degeneration doctrine.
    The second Valentín, although the most notable, is not the
only example in the series of Galdós's disengagement with contemporary ideas on congenital degeneration. Another example is
provided by the portrayal, in *Torquemada en la hoguera*, of the first
Valentín, the mathematical genius who dies from meningitis as a
child. In spite of the fact that Valentín displays 'degenerative

traits', the text does not describe here a case of pathological inheritance. The association of genius and insanity/degeneration was established by the Italian criminologist Cesare Lombroso in his work *Genio e Follio* (1863), where he ascribed to the genius the same degenerative symptoms that produced alienation in the criminal. In this respect, it is significant that the first Valentín, in spite of his angelic qualities,[76] is also referred to as a monster on several occasions by the narrator of *Torquemada en la hoguera*, which may be related to Lombroso's association of genius with monstrosity and degeneration. Interestingly, Lombroso is mentioned in *Torquemada en el purgatorio* by the *pedante* Zárate, one of Rafael's friends. As the narrator points out: '[Zárate], que estaba al corriente de lo moderno, espigando todo el saber en periódicos y revistas, sin profundizar nada, desembuchó las opiniones de Lombroso [. . .], que Torquemada aprobó plenamente, haciéndolas suyas' (*OC*, 1042). The fact that Galdós uses an unattractive and shallow character like Zárate to voice Lombroso's theories, which, like all modern fashionable theories have an impact on the gullible Torquemada, is indicative of his mocking approach to Lombroso's doctrine. José Luis Peset and Mariano Peset have argued that Lombroso's theories did not have a profound effect in Spain, particularly in the Spanish realist novel, where they were not assimilated nor admitted in their entirety.[77] It is significant, in this respect, that genius as a kind of degeneration tends to be disregarded in contemporary Spanish medical writings. In *Torquemada en la hoguera*, Galdós introduces the issue of genius but does not make any explicit comments that might link it with Lombrosian doctrine. Interestingly, the following year, in *Angel Guerra* (1890–1), Galdós would appear to associate genius with hereditary degeneration through the portrayal of Leré's family, where the father is said to be an alcoholic who has produced a genius and several 'monsters', as Leré describes them. Although a possible link between the father's alcoholism and the degenerate progeny is suggested in the novel, the fact that there is an element of humour in the description of the alcoholic father lessens the force of such an association.[78] In *Torquemada en la hoguera*, the link between genius/monstrosity and a morbid heredity is much less clear.

The fact that the first Valentín is afflicted with meningitis is not associated with congenital degeneration either. The anxieties sparked by meningitis are reflected in the numerous references to the disease as a cause of infant mortality in contemporary debates. Public health experts taking part in the various International Congresses of Hygiene and Demography frequently produced statistics to that effect. It must be remembered that meningitis was cited among the degenerative diseases resulting from hereditary alcoholism by the French psychiatrist Legrain, who had an influence on Spanish degenerationist discourse, as Cervera's 'Alcoholismo y civilización' shows. Furthermore, in keeping with Morel's notion of 'polymorphous heredity', the disease could be the result of the hereditary transmission of any pathological condition. The issue of alcoholism does not figure, however, in *Torquemada en la hoguera*. Similarly, Toquemada's epilepsy is discarded as a predisposing factor. Indeed, Torquemada is shown to suffer his first epileptic fit straight after Valentín's death: therefore, epilepsy is presented as a direct consequence of his son's death. In his portrayal of Valentín's disease, Galdós, rather, seems to endorse the contemporary belief voiced by Hauser and other hygienists of the period: that an excess of study and an abnormal cerebral activity – both seen to be the inevitable consequences of progress and the hectic pace of modern urban life – could be possible causes of cerebrospinal diseases. These ideas are echoed in the episode when Quevedo, after examining the sick Valentín, tells Torquemada: 'Ya le he dicho a usted que tuviera mucho cuidado con este fenómeno de chico. ¡Tanto estudiar, tanto saber, un desarrollo cerebral disparatado!' (*OC*, 915). Tía Roma seems to reiterate this idea, in her colloquial language, when she claims that Valentín's illness is due to 'una reventazón del talento en la cabeza' (*OC*, 922).[79] In this respect, it is significant that Galdós should present Torquemada's two sons as posited at two opposite poles: whereas the second Valentín's degeneration is equated with savagery and seen as a result of lack of civilization, the first Valentín is portrayed as a product of the degenerative state caused by progress.

In 'El siglo XIX considerado bajo el punto de vista médico-social', Hauser drew attention to the rapid increase of nervous disorders and mental disease in most European countries in the last quarter of the nineteenth century.[80] Hauser expressed his concern that the demands of modern civilization had led to 'un estado degenerativo [. . .] de la raza humana'. According to this hygienist, the immense development of the human brain in modern societies had been reached at the expense of an incredible expenditure of nervous energy, which had resulted in 'generaciones con mayor desarrollo del sistema nervioso, pero también de menor resistencia vital y más expuestas a todo el cortejo de enfermedades [. . .] del centro cerebro-espinal, tan frecuentes en nuestra época'.[81] In Hauser's view, one powerful factor contributing to 'exaltar y agotar la sensibilidad nerviosa' was the education system in public and private schools and, in particular, the continuous imposition of greater intellectual work on the young.[82] Other hygienists of the period voiced very similar ideas regarding the effects of an excess of intellectual work on the nervous system. Three years before the publication of *Torquemada en la hoguera*, Fernández Caro stated:

> Sobrecargar de estudios la enseñanza [. . .] creyendo que con esto se ilustra más a la juventud, es un error que ha suscitado una unánime protesta por parte de todos los hombres de ciencia. El ejercicio excesivo de la inteligencia conduce a la exaltación mental, al empobrecimiento orgánico, y determina en muchos casos verdaderas psicosis.[83]

The point was reiterated in the various International Congresses of Hygiene and Demography held in the 1880s and 1890s, in particular, the IV Congress, held at Geneva,[84] and the IX Congress of Madrid. At the latter Congress, Bernabé Malo, making specific reference to meningitis, noted that one of the causes of the disease was what he called 'caquexia[85] urbana', by which he meant the 'excesivo consumo de energías orgánicas en un vivir azaroso de *pseudo-progreso*'.[86] Significantly, he also referred to the 'alcoholismo crónico' of the predecessors as a cause of meningitis.[87] Thus, although excess of study was considered as a determining factor of the disease, the physiological element was never ruled out, in keeping with the emphasis placed by contemporary scientific discourse on organic, or physiological, causes of degenerative diseases. As it was believed, the nervous system was weakened by a hereditary predisposition, which made the sufferer more vulnerable to any external influences. In accordance with ideas expressed by Hauser and other contemporaries, in the *Torquemada* series, Galdós underplays the congenital explanation, stressing instead environmental factors associated with the excesses of civilization and industrial progress and the stark competition of modern urban life. The case of the first Valentín is, as we have seen, an obvious example of this. Within this wider framework, the root cause of the characters' degeneration is shown to be linked to personal circumstances: that is, circumstances which make an individual's condition a particular case history, as the portrayal of Rafael del Aguila demonstrates. The texts seem to indicate that the socio-economic progress propounded by materialist utilitarian voices had been counterproductive, leading to ill health and degeneracy. Utilitarianism, for all its emphasis on waste, is shown to be generating more 'waste'.

Like the first Valentín, it could be argued that Rafael del Aguila is presented as another victim of the 'new' nervous afflictions that Hauser linked to the over-expenditure of nervous energy inherent in modern civilization. More specifically, Rafael's nervous disorders – which the text of *Torquemada en el purgatorio* suggests are related to hysteria – are presented by Galdós as the direct result of his personal circumstances, which eventually lead him to commit suicide. It is made abundantly clear in the series that the causes of Rafael's condition are psychological and, to an extent, sociological. Although it is after the birth of Valentín that Rafael's nervous illness begins to manifest itself in violent fits, he is shown to suffer from what the narrator calls 'desórdenes neuróticos' (*OC*, 1043) and 'trastornos cerebrales' (*OC*, 1058) from an earlier stage in the narrative when his sister Fidela marries Torquemada. The social alienation Rafael had suffered as a result of his blindness, which was to a degree replaced by the care and attention provided by his sisters, is now compounded by his isolation from his own family. The emotional ties uniting him with his sisters are weakened after Fidela's union with Torquemada. This represents a blow to Rafael's aristocratic pride. Also, if we agree with Ricardo Gullón's interpretation of the relationship between Fidela and Rafael as semi-incestuous, albeit in an unconscious way,[88] it would be possible to argue that Fidela's marriage to Torquemada would have been a cause of affliction, independently of what it represents socially. But the main cause of Rafael's emotional upset, and the trigger for his nervous condition, is the birth of the second Valentín, to whom he feels he has lost the love and attention of his sisters. Significantly, on one occasion Rafael refers to his attacks as 'accesos de envidia' (*OC*, 1090).

A number of symptoms presented by Rafael during his attacks correspond to what were believed by contemporary doctors to be

manifestations of hysteria, notably the brutal nature of the outbursts themselves (described as 'salvajes arrechuchos' by the
narrator (*OC*, 1090)), and the lack of control over his will and
actions. When commenting on Rafael's brutal and irrational
aversion towards Valentín, the narrator writes: 'El sentimiento de
su impotencia para vencer aquel insano impulso era tan afectivo
[*sic*] y claro en su alma como el del espanto que le causaba' (*OC*,
1090). This point is strengthened by Rafael himself when he
admits: 'Si el ataque me coge con mi sobrinito en brazos, necesito
echarme con la voluntad cinturones de bronce para no dejarme
caer sobre el pobre niño y ahogarle bajo mi cuerpo' (*OC*, 1091).
Rafael continues to say that he fears that a time will come when he
will be unable to control his will and consummate Valentín's
murder (*OC*, 1091). As Aldaraca has noted in respect of hysteria:
'la represión de las emociones la paga el cuerpo. El lenguaje
corporal de la histeria es un lenguaje de dolor físico [. . .]. El
histérico expresa con el cuerpo lo que no puede expresar me-
diante el lenguaje hablado. El lenguaje corporal dice lo indec-
ible'.[89] This could be applied to the case of Rafael, who needs to
repress the resentment and jealousy he feels towards his nephew
Valentín.

In nineteenth-century scientific discourse, the inability to control one's emotions was linked to the instability that characterized
mental disease. It was also a reflection of the supposed lack of
control and equilibrium and the changeability associated with the
feminine nature.[90] In a speech delivered in the Real Academia de
Medicina de Granada in 1893 (the year before the publication of
Torquemada en el Purgatorio), the speaker commented on the
hysterical woman's lack of will to control her emotions, drawing
attention to the fact that these women 'son impelidas a la
realización de actos extremos o reprobados por la moral'.[91]
Similarly, in an article of 1882 written for the women's journal *La
Guirnalda* – in which Galdós published articles and novels – its
author observed the precariousness of women's emotional balance, likening the hysterical's condition to a packet of dynamite:
'inofensivo mientras sus partículas están en equilibrio, terrible
cuando se conmueve'.[92] In this respect, it is significant that Rafael
should compare the onset of his violent outbursts to an explosive
going off. He says: 'yo no sé lo que me pasa ni cómo empieza el
endiablado ataque. Estalla de súbito como un explosivo. Me
invade todo el sistema nervioso en menos tiempo que empleo en

decirlo' (*OC*, 1091). Other symptoms shown by Rafael, related to hysteria, include the inability to stand up or walk (Rafael says: 'me vuelvo de trapo y no sé tenerme' (*OC*, 1092)), muscle contractions, epileptic convulsions (*OC*, 1092), the choking sensation that he feels when he holds the child (*OC*, 1090), and his 'ganas ardientes de llorar' (*OC*, 1090). Similarly, Rafael's irrational and uncontrolled laughing 'fits' – the first symptom that draws Cruz's attention to Rafael's problem (*OC*, 1024–8) – as well as the melancholy and sadness of which he is often a victim, and the indifference and disdain he feels towards others (*OC*, 1031), have also been seen as manifestations of the disease.[93]

The connection between Rafael's nervous disorders and hysteria – the 'female disease' *par excellence*[94] – is also suggested by Fidela's proposition that Rafael should be taken to Paris in order to be examined by Charcot, 'el primer sabio de Europa en enfermedades cerebrales' (*OC*, 1028). Jean Martin Charcot (1825–93), a French physioneurologist, was the first of the great masters of the science of hysteria. He was the director of the Salpêtrière, a Parisian hospital for nervous diseases that reached international reputation in the 1870s and 1880s. His works began to be published in 1872, and there is evidence that they were not unknown to Galdós.[95] It is interesting that when Cruz agrees with her sister's suggestion to take Rafael to see a specialist, insisting that 'no podemos consentir que tome cuerpo esa neurosis', Torquemada objects to what in his view is an extravagant idea. Thus he says in a mocking tone: '¿Esa qué . . .? ¡Ah! Ya, neurosis, *paparruchosis* . . .' (*OC*, 1028). Pérez Bautista, in his study of disease in the Spanish realist novel, remarked that the contemporary scientific ignorance about these 'new' diseases – which, as Hauser had noted, emerged towards the end of the nineteenth century – led to a slack use of the term 'neurosis', and to its application to all kinds of nervous disorders, including hysteria.[96] By making Torquemada refer to Rafael's nervous illness as 'paparruchas' (medicalizing the term by using the humorous 'paparruchosis'), Galdós may be ridiculing his ignorance. This could also be read, however, as the author's compliance with Torquemada's view: like the protagonist of the series, Galdós may be playing down the contemporary obsession with nervous disorders and their over-use in medical diagnosis, when, in reality, they still remained a scientific mystery.[97]

In *Leçons sur les maladies du système nerveux*, a Spanish version of which was published in 1882, Charcot discarded the belief that hysteria was specifically a female disorder relating to disturbances in the reproductive system, claiming that the symptoms of the disease also occurred in men. He developed a theory that hysteria had psychological origins, although he did not rule out the hereditary predisposition of the hysteric. Hysteria originated, according to Charcot, in a lesion in an area of the brain (the cerebellum), caused by a debilitated nervous system, for which a tainted heredity was to blame. Spanish doctors, more conservative than Charcot, endorsed, in their great majority, the thesis that hysteria had a genital rather than a neurological origin, and was necessarily related to women.[98] It could be said that by linking Rafael with hysteria, Galdós is breaking away from the ideas prevailing in Spanish medical circles. It needs to be noted, however, that Rafael is depicted as a feminine character, which would call into question Galdós's eagerness to undermine the association of hysteria with women. When Rafael is first introduced to Torquemada, the narrator comments on his 'cutis blanquísimo de nítida cera', and his 'mano[s] de mujer, de una pulcritud extremada' (*OC*, 948). Shortly after, Rafael's impeccable appearance is emphasized: 'era el tal una figura delicada y distinguidísima, cara hermosa, manos cinceladas, pies de mujer, de una forma intachable' (*OC*, 948). Moreover, Rafael's exaggerated cleanliness, also highlighted in the text, compounds his feminine image. It is also important to consider that the passive life Rafael is forced to live, because of his blindness, is not too different from the constraints suffered by so many women at the end of the nineteenth century, particularly in bourgeois households. Notwithstanding the contemporary biological bias, there was an awareness among some doctors and psychiatrists of the significance of psychological and sociological factors in the genesis of hysteria. In this regard, enforced passivity and, similarly, sexual repression, were seen as possible causes of hysteria, as well as any condition of emotional tension.

A link is suggested in *Torquemada en el purgatorio* between Rafael's neurotic derangement and his suicide at the end of the novel. Suicide was listed by late nineteenth-century hygienists – along with alcoholism, insanity, criminality, prostitution and mendicity – as a social pathology (*una enfermedad del cuerpo social*). The incidence of these pathologies, often conceptualized in terms of a plague, was regarded as evidence that society was diseased, in other words, as being symptomatic of the moral and racial degeneration of the population.[99] Critics of the *Torquemada* novels have often ignored the wider socio-cultural implications of Rafael's suicide, tending to interpret his death as symbolic not only of the death of his family line,[100] but also of the sociological phenomenon of the disappearance of the aristocracy itself.[101] Like other manifestations of degeneration, suicide was seen as a drain on the economy, as it detracted from economic and social progress. Jesús Sarabia y Pardo, for instance, regarded suicide as an 'ataque [. . .] contra una existencia que origina en ocasiones determinadas notorios beneficios a la familia y al Estado' and, quoting J. J. Rousseau described it as a 'robo hecho al género humano'.[102] Rafael's death does not represent, however, a waste of capital, as due to his blindness his life is far from being productive. One can read irony into Galdós's portrayal of a character who is a victim of disease and degeneration but who is, essentially, an economic burden.

The fact that the text suggests that Rafael is an individual with a specific case history seems to indicate Galdós's disagreement with the contemporary stress laid on the physiological origins of degenerative diseases. Although there is some information provided about Rafael's parents in *Torquemada en el purgatorio*, this information is not relevant to the issue of hereditary degeneration: the author does not offer any details regarding Rafael's ancestors as the possible root cause of his condition, or, indeed, of his sister Fidela's. Fidela's weak constitution and her anaemic complexion are linked, rather, to her aristocratic upbringing. As the narrator points out: 'su color anémico [. . .] denunciaba [. . .] a la señorita de estirpe, pura sangre, sin cruzamientos que vivifican, enclenque de nacimiento y desmedrada luego por una educación de estufa' (*OC*, 946). Moreover, the Aguilas older sister, Cruz, is not made to suffer from any degenerative disease – another example of the lack of consistency and systematicity with which the issue of degeneration is treated in the *Torquemada* series. The same argument could be made regarding the protagonist of the series himself. By making Torquemada's epileptic attacks take place after the deaths of the first Valentín and Fidela, the author makes it plain that the fits are a direct result of the emotional impact that these two deaths had on the protagonist, rather than the inevitable consequences of hereditary epilepsy.

In contrast to Emile Zola, who wrote twenty novels centred on the pathological history of a family throughout five generations, here there is no complex and perfectly elaborate genealogical tree. Also, we are not told, as we are in Zola, where all the various diseases afflicting the family members originated. In most cases, we do not know anything about the parents of the characters marked by degeneration. In those cases where information is provided, the degenerative traits of a character are not shown to be the result of a diseased inheritance. Indeed, possible links between a morbid condition and heredity are dismissed. What I am concerned to demonstrate is that, in spite of Galdós's obvious concern with the burning issue of degeneration and his profound knowledge of the debates circulating at the time, he is not interested in tracing the history of a family whose members have suffered the effects of a predecessor's degeneration through several generations in the methodical and precise way that Zola had done. Although the *Torquemada* series echoes some commonly held views on the issue of degeneration, Galdós does not uphold degeneration doctrine in a whole-hearted way, and often challenges stock assumptions of the time.[103]

NOTES

[1] Galdós's private library in Las Palmas contains a series of books on racial degeneration, which reflects the author's interest in the issue. It is also worthy of note that during one of the *tertulias* that take place at the Gravelinas palace, Rafael brings up the issue of 'las nuevas teorías de la degeneración', as the narrator observes (*OC*, 1094).

[2] See Ricardo Campos Marín, José Martínez Pérez and Rafael Huertas García-Alejo, *Los ilegales de la naturaleza. Medicina y degeneracionismo en la España de la Restauración (1876–1923)* (Madrid: C.S.I.C., 2001), pp. 18–32. In this regard, Pick has also pointed out that, in spite of the environment being regarded as a key factor in degeneration, there is a sense, in Morel's *Treatise*, that the degenerate's family tree is immutable and so is its journey towards extinction: see Daniel Pick, *Faces of Degeneration* (Cambridge: Cambridge University Press, 1993), p. 101.

[3] These ideas were repeated three decades later by Magnan in *Leçons cliniques sur les maladies mentales* (1887), where the author states: 'El hecho general, para él [Morel] es la transmisión de las afecciones mentales por agravamiento progresivo de la enfermedad en los descendientes. Así, los ascendientes se dan a conocer por la exageración del temperamento nervioso, dando lugar a histéricos,

epilépticos, hipocondríacos. Estos [. . .] procrearán alienados y estos últimos tendrán en su descendencia imbéciles, idiotas; los cuales, en última instancia, son gravados por la esterilidad'. Quoted by Rafael Huertas, 'Valentín Magnan y la teoría de la degeneración', *Revista de la Asociación Española de Neuropsiquiatría*, V, 14 (1985), 361–7, 362.

4   The most obvious example in the *Torquemada* series is the second Valentín, who is described as having a 'complexión raquítica' (*OC*, 1083). Anxieties about racial degeneration are also voiced by Donoso when he talks about 'la juventud encanijada que anda por ahí' (*OC*, 965). The issue of rickets is raised by Galdós in other novels. In *Angel Guerra*, talking about the nephew of the priest Virones, the narrator comments: 'Tenía todo el desarrollo propio de sus seis años, cosa rara en estos tiempos de raquitismo': *Angel Guerra*, 2 vols (Madrid: Alianza, 1986), vol. 2, p. 536. Similarly, in *La desheredada*, Isidora's son is born with rickets.

5   Rafael Cervera y Barat, *Alcoholismo y civilización* (1898), in Antonio M. Rey González (ed.), *Estudios médico-sociales sobre marginados en la España del siglo XIX* (Madrid: Ministerio de Sanidad y Consumo, 1990), pp. 107–28, 114.

6   The Italian criminologist Cesare Lombroso regarded genius, both scientific and artistic, as another sign of abnormality linked to degeneration. Becoming influential in Spain in the 1880s and reaching a high point in the mid 1890s, Lombroso's scientific investigations on criminality highlighted hereditary alcoholism as a major cause of degeneration. See Luis Maristanyi, 'Lombroso y España: Nuevas consideraciones', *Anales de Literatura Española*, 2 (1983), Universidad de Alicante, 361–81; and José Luis Peset and Mariano Peset, *Lombroso y la escuela positivista italiana* (Madrid: C.S.I.C., 1975). As we shall see, although Galdós was clearly familiar with Lombrosian doctrine, he did not subscribe to its premises, disengaging from the facile biological determinism which characterizes it.

7   This point was stressed, for instance, by Angel Fernández Caro (*Los deberes de la sociedad ante los intereses de la Higiene. Discursos leídos en la sesión inaugural del año académico de 1886–1887 en la Sociedad Española de Higiene, celebrada el día 27 de noviembre de 1886* [Madrid: Imprenta de Enrique Teodoro, 1886], pp. 3–43) and Philippe Hauser ('El siglo XIX considerado bajo el punto de vista médico-social', *Revista de España* 101 [1884], 202–24 and 333–58), both writing shortly before the publication of the first novel of the series. W. H. Shoemaker has noted (*The Novelistic Art of Galdós*, 3 vols [Valencia: Albatrós Hispanófila, 1980], vol. 2) Galdós's connections with the *Revista de España*, an influential journal which he edited in the early 1870s and in which he published serially some of his novels. In relation to Galdós's links with the *Revista de España*, see also Peter B. Goldman, 'Galdós and the politics of reconciliation, *Anales Galdosianos*, IV (1969), 74–87; and Brian J. Dendle, 'Albareda, Galdós and the *Revista de España* (1868–73), in Clara E. Lida and Iris M. Zavala (eds), *La revolución de 1868: Historia, pensamiento, literatura* (New York: Las Américas, 1970), pp. 362–77.

8   Ricardo Campos Marín, 'La teoría de la degeneración y la medicina social en España en el cambio de siglo', *Llull*, 21, 41 (1998), 333–56, 337.

9   The first of these Congresses took place in Brussels in 1852 and the last in Washington in 1922.

10 Hauser, 'El siglo XIX', 355.

11 Tomás Gallego y Gallego, 'Mortalidad comparada de Europa', in *Actas y Memorias del IX Congreso Internacional de Higiene y Demografía. Madrid, 10–17 abril de 1898.* Enrique Salcedo Ginestral (ed.). 14 vols (Madrid: Imprenta de Ricardo Rojas, 1900), vol. 13, pp. 60–8, 60. Similarly, the V International Congress, held in The Hague, includes a letter from the utilitarian public health reformer Edwin Chadwick, who was unable to attend the Congress due to old age. In it, Chadwick emphasized the economic value of human life and the need to prevent excessive sickness and premature mortality among the waged classes, urging members of the Congress to examine the waste that these represented in their respective countries: see *Cinquième Congrès international d'hygiène et de démographie à La Haye* (du 21 au 27 août 1884). Comptes rendus et mémoires publiés par le Secrétaire Général. 2 tomes, La Haye, 1884, vol. 1, pp. 132–3.

12 Angel Fernández Caro, *Los deberes de la sociedad*, p. 17. In another speech, delivered fourteen years later, Fernández Caro reiterated this idea, establishing a link between 'salud' and 'capital'. According to this hygienist, 'la Higiene es cara, pero no más que la enfermedad y que la muerte', as in his view, 'no hay dispendio mayor que el de la vida humana': 'Discurso del académico [. . .] Angel Fernández-Caro y Nouvilas en contestación al discurso presentado por M. Tolosa, "Concepto y fines de la higiene popular"', in *Discursos leídos en la Real Academia de Medicina para la recepción pública del académico electo Manuel de Tolosa Latour* (Madrid: Est. Tip. de la Viuda e Hijos de Tello, 1900), pp. 47–68, 56, 54. In order to reinforce his ideas Fernández-Caro refers to the findings of European public health experts, such as Chadwick, who 'han hecho un estudio de la contabilidad de la vida humana, y saben al dedillo lo que cuesta una enfermedad, [. . .], lo que significa para la producción y la riqueza pública la muerte de un individuo en la plenitud de su juventud y de su vigor (p. 56).

13 Fernández Caro, *Los deberes de la sociedad*, p. 5.

14 Ibid., pp. 4–5. Donoso's association of social order and material progress with hygiene in *Torquemada en la cruz* is noteworthy in this respect: *OC*, 959.

15 Tomás Valera y Jiménez, 'La salud nacional es la riqueza nacional', *El Siglo Médico*, 39 (13 November 1892), 732–5, 735. Resorting to the science of statistics to strengthen his views, Valera y Jiménez stated that: 'Cuantos se dedican [. . .] a las estadísticas [. . .] nos enseñan de un modo indubitable que se pierden muchos millones de riqueza con las enfermedades y las muertes prematuras, haciendo deducciones y comparaciones entre el hombre sano y el enfermo, entre los gastos y lo que dejan de producir y de ganar' (735).

16 Rosa Ballester and Emilio Balaguer, 'La infancia como valor y como

problema en las luchas sanitarias de principios de siglo en España',
Dynamis, 15 (1995), 177–92, 180.

[17] This point was made, for instance, by Fernández Caro, *Los deberes de la sociedad*, p. 17.

[18] Ibid., p. 20. Children were literally given a price, as if they were merchandise. Some years later, at the beginning of the twentieth century, a doctor on children's hygiene commented: 'Aparte del valor moral afectivo con que los padres apreciamos a nuestros hijos, existe otro valor numérico que los economistas han concedido a cada niño. Os causará asombro a vosotras, que no cambiaríais vuestros hijos por todos los tesoros del mundo, saber que hay quien se ha atrevido a poner un precio de *vil metal* a cada criatura; pero el hecho es positivo y conviene consignarlo': Andrés Martínez Vargas, *Nuestras madres y el engrandecimiento patrio* (Barcelona: Establecimiento Tipográfico de Jaime Vives, 1906), p. 20. The author also includes a table specifying the monetary value of children between the ages of one and five, and compares child mortality with the loss of 'copiosos ríos de oro' (p. 20).

[19] It is noteworthy, in this respect, that Galdós's personal friend Manuel Tolosa Latour, a famous specialist in children's medicine and author of a number of scientific works on children's hygiene, participated in various debates on child mortality that took place during the IX Congress of Hygiene and Demography.

[20] 'Fomento de la vitalidad en España', in *Actas del IX Congreso Internacional de Higiene y Demografía*, vol. 13, pp. 46–50, 46. Many of the papers published in the transactions include statistical tables of birth, marriage and mortality rates. In the last three decades of the nineteenth century, there were a large number of publications on the theme of population growth and hygiene's role in preventing disease and death. Further to the transactions of the Congresses of Hygiene and Demography, monographs were written on the issue, as well as numerous periodical publications, such as *El Siglo Médico* and the *Revista de la Sociedad Española de Higiene*. Non-specialized Spanish journals of the period, like *La Correspondencia, El Liberal, El Imparcial, La Epoca, El Globo* and *Heraldo de Madrid*, also included articles in connection with hygiene and demography. Furthermore, the 'Dirección de Beneficencia y Sanidad' published during this time periodicals whose main aim was the provision of statistics on birth and mortality rates: see E. Sánchez Rubio, *Bibliographie espagnole d'Hygiène et de Démographie*, in *Actas del IX Congreso Internacional de Higiene y Demografía*, vol. 12, pp. 31–55.

[21] Fernández Caro, *Los deberes de la sociedad*, p. 18. Fernández Caro believed that the State should promote marriage, affirming that 'El Estado [. . .] debe hacer lo posible para que el matrimonio sea un derecho general' (p. 19). He went on to say that '[El Estado] debe impedir la vagancia, perseguir el juego, castigar la embriaguez, evitar la prostitución y destruir todos los alicientes con que el vicio aparta al hombre de la vida metódica y regular del trabajo y del santo amor de

la familia y del hogar' (pp. 18–19). Marriage was used, of course, as an instrument of social control, a means of achieving social order and stability.

22 Ibid., p. 9. The individual's duties towards society were also stressed by Valera y Jiménez, 732–5.

23 Later in the series, in *Torquemada y San Pedro*, Torquemada seems to internalize Donoso's lessons when he insists that by converting the external debt into internal debt he will be benefiting the *colectividad*, as he will be serving the interests of the State.

24 Contemporary hygienists, aware of the threats posed by child disease and mortality, often stressed the importance of bringing up robust children. One commented that: 'El nacimiento de niños robustos y su feliz desarrollo es problema de grandísimo interés, y merecedor como el que más de ocupar la atención de médicos, sociólogos y estadistas': Bernabé Malo, 'Causas que contribuyen a la mortalidad de los niños. Medios de remediarlas. Estadísticas comparativas', in *Actas del IX Congreso Internacional de Higiene y Demografía*, vol. 6, pp. 38–51, 38.

25 In this respect, the French psychiatrist J. E. D. Esquirol (*Tratado completo de las enagenaciones mentales*, 2 vols [Madrid: Imprenta del Colegio de Surdo-Mudos, 1847], pp. 154, 155. Tr. by Raimundo de Monasterio y Correa) pointed out that '[e]l cretinismo es una variedad notable del idiotismo' and that 'los cretinenses presentan los mismos caracteres, las mismas variedades de incapacidad intelectual, de insensibilidad física y moral que se observan en los idiotas'. Critics have tended to refer to Valentín's condition as 'imbecility' or 'idiocy', some of them invariably. In fact, these were seen to represent two different degrees of degeneration. The public health expert Juan Giné y Partagás, for instance ('El idiotismo o imbecilidad moral. Discurso pronunciado en la sesión inaugural del "Ateneo Graciense", celebrada el día 12 de octubre de 1895', in *Obras escogidas* [Barcelona: Tipografía la Académica, 1903], pp. 529–45), clarified that '*idiotismo* es el grado mayor de la *imbecilidad*' (p. 539). Quoting another doctor, he drew a line between *imbecilidad*, 'que comprende los individuos [. . .] que poseen aún cierto grado de inteligencia' and *idiotismo*, 'que reúne a los seres en quienes la suspensión del desarrollo intelectual llega a sus últimos límites' (p. 535). Similarly, the eminent forensic doctor Pedro Mata established a clear difference between these two degrees of mental degeneration. Mata also observed that the imbecile does not present the external deformities that characterize idiotism: as noted by José María Esquerdo in *Locos que no lo parecen. Conferencia dada por el Dr Esquerdo en la Facultad de Medicina* (Madrid: Oficina Tipográfica del Hospicio, 1880), pp. 6–8. It is worth noting that Mata is mentioned by Galdós in *Fortunata y Jacinta* (2 vols, ed. by Francisco Caudet [Madrid: Cátedra, 1983], vol. 2, p. 144). Galdós also knew Esquerdo, a prominent psychiatrist, whom he would have met through Tolosa Latour, as Gordon Minter has observed in 'The medical background to Galdós' *La desheredada*', *Anales Galdosianos*, VII (1972), 67–77, 68.

26   Pick, pp. 45–6. As Pick has noted, the problem of cretinism was one that attracted other realist authors in Europe. Among these was Balzac, who dealt with the issue in *The Country Doctor* (1833), and Dickens, who wrote a piece on the treatment of idiocy for *Household Words*, VII (4 June 1853), 313–17, a journal that he edited.

27   Morel, while admitting that cretinism could be congenital or acquired, had stressed the role of pathological heredity in the production of degenerates (see Pick, 48). Later in the century, and within the more specific context of Spain, both heredity and environmental factors were seen as possible causes of cretinism. In this respect, see, for instance, Fernández Caro y Nouvilas, '¿Cuál es el concepto científico de las causas del cretinismo y qué medios pueden proponerse para combatir ese mal?', in *Estudios Críticos sobre el 6 Congreso Internacional de Higiene y Demografía de Viena* (Madrid: Imprenta de Infantería de Marina, 1888), pp. 385–90; and Mariano Baglietto, 'Algunos datos estadísticos acerca del bocio y el cretinismo en la provincia de Asturias', in *Actas del IX Congreso Internacional de Higiene y Demografía*, vol. 12, pp. 241–3.

28   Morel, 'An analysis of a treatise on the degenerations, physical, intellectual and moral of the human race, and the causes which produce their unhealthy varieties with notes and remarks by the translator Edwin Wing M. D.', *Medical Circular*, 10–12 (1857–8), as quoted by Pick, p. 48, n.33.

29   Pick, pp. 47–8.

30   In this respect, a contributor to *El Siglo Médico* warned that a diseased inheritance 'priva [. . .] a la familia del descendiente sano y a la patria de miembros útiles, gravando a una y otra en el sentido utilitario, pues que el enfermo no solamente no produce, sino que, además, gasta, conduciendo a la ruina, a la degeneración y, por último, hasta a la extinción de la raza': see Baldomero González Alvarez, 'Higiene profiláctica del niño respecto a la herencia', *El Siglo Médico*, 50 (30 August 1903), 582–5. Similarly, Fernández-Caro y Nouvilas ('Discurso [. . .] en contestación', p. 59) talks about the *gravamen* that non-useful citizens represent, to the detriment of the public good. The same point was to be made over a decade later by Fernández Juncos, who also refers to these members of the population as 'material [no] deseable para la obra del progreso del país'. Writing in 1913, Fernández Juncos, not surprisingly, goes on to promote the implementation of repressive measures (such as sterilization and segregation) in order to control the procreation of degenerates: see Manuel Fernández Juncos (ed.), *Conferencias dominicales dadas en la Biblioteca Insular de Puerto Rico. Temas: escuelas públicas, higiene, delincuencia, etc.* (San Juan de Puerto Rico: Bureau of Supplies, Ports and Transportation, 1913), pp. 16–17 and 19–20. It is noteworthy that this book is in Galdós's personal library and contains a dedication to Galdós from the author.

31   Torquemada's aversion to poetry, a reflection of his utilitarian spirit, is noted by Galdós at various points in the series.

32   Quoted by Pick, 47.

33 In an article entitled 'Idiots', Dickens – who, like Morel, based his arguments on the research carried out by Dr Guggenbühl – argued against the popular notion of an idiot as a 'hopeless, irreclaimable, unimprovable being'. He continued to say that although this image had tended to dominate studies in idiocy, a closer examination of the issue proved that the idiot's condition could be improved to an extent. Dickens drew attention to Dr Guggenbühl's conviction that there was a dormant mind in cretins, which led the latter to make these beings the object of his investigations. See Charles Dickens, 'Idiots', *Household Worlds*, 7 (1853), 313–17.

34 Quoted by Pick, p. 47. Following in Morel's footsteps, Fernández-Caro y Nouvilas ('¿Cuál es el concepto científico de las causas del cretinismo?', p. 390) drew a line between complete and incomplete cretinism when he asserted: 'Hay en el día muchos establecimientos pedagógicos dedicados a la instrucción de niños cretinos, y sus resultados son brillantes [. . .]; pero, cuando el cretinismo es completo, todo cuanto se intente para su curación es completamente infructuoso'. In this respect, Pick (p. 47) has observed the contradictions surrounding the conception of the degenerate: the fatalistic resonances of Morel's description of cretinism need to be seen within the context of contemporary medicine's commitment, in other respects, to the social amelioration of the condition of the cretin.

35 Tom Bell ('Evolutionary theory in the *novelas contemporáneas* of Benito Pérez Galdós' [unpublished Ph.D. thesis, University of Sheffield, 2003], p. 131) has noted Galdós's allusion, in his Academy speech 'La sociedad presente como materia novelable', to language as 'la marca de la raza'. Being unique to the human species, verbal communication became an important area of discussion in the late nineteenth-century Darwinian debate.

36 In respect of Valentín's animality, it is interesting to note, as Pick (p. 47) has, that despite the etymology of the term 'cretin' being linked to the word 'Christian', it was in effect the human condition of these unfortunate individuals that was questioned. It is thus significant and also highly ironic that the 'savage' Valentín was born on Christmas Eve.

37 Jose Harris ('Between civic virtue and Social Darwinism: The concept of the residuum', in David Englander and Rosemary O'Day (eds), *Retrieved Riches: Social Investigation in Britain* [Aldershot: Scolar Press, 1995], pp. 67–87, 67–8) has argued that, following the popularization of Darwinist evolutionary theory, the urban poor were increasingly seen as 'primitive tribes' and 'savages', isolated from the 'civilized' by a permanent 'hereditary gap'.

38 It has been observed by Pick (pp. 37–44) that although 'inferiority', 'savagery' and 'moral pathology' were seen as essentially 'non-European' characteristics, serving to emphasize European cultural hegemony and a notion of cultural unity 'at home', the fear of degeneration in the 'civilized' world always threatened the legitimacy of the imperial discourse that boasted superiority over colonial races.

39 Ibid., pp. 37–44.

40   Teresa Fuentes Peris, *Images of Filth: Deviancy and Social Control in the Novels of Galdós* (Liverpool: Liverpool University Press, 2003).

41   Neurasthenia, a nervous disorder associated with the pressures of the modern world, was frequent among the well-to-do, often being linked with middle-class male intellectuals, businessmen and professionals: see Elaine Showalter, *The Female Malady: Women, Madness and English Culture, 1830–1980* (London: Virago, 1987), p. 35. Neurasthenia is one of the nervous diseases linked to the demands of modern life to which Hauser refers in his study (see 'El siglo XIX', 206–7).

42   See, for instance, Gustavo Correa, *El simbolismo religioso en las novelas de Pérez Galdós* (Madrid: Gredos, 1962), p. 144. Similarly, for Geraldine Scanlon ('Torquemada: "Becerro de oro"', *Modern Language Notes*, 91, 1 [1976], 264–76), the second Valentín is symbolic of the desert that the bourgeoisie was deemed to have created with their blind economic values: 'a symbol of a future born of a present devoted only to the material: like Christ, he brings news of a new world' (273). Within the more specific context of social class, Valentín's abnormality has been seen as representative of the impossibility of uniting the aristocratic and the plebeian (Joaquín Casalduero, *Vida y obra de Galdós*, 2nd edn [Madrid: Gredos, 1961], p. 117); or as symbolizing the rise of a commercial class and the decay of the aristocracy (Robert J. Weber, 'Galdós's preliminary sketches for *Torquemada y San Pedro*', *Bulletin of Hispanic Studies*, 44 [1967], 16–27, 26; and Mac Gregor O'Brien, 'Las religiones de Torquemada', *Discurso Literario*, 9, 2 [1985], 111–19, 118). Furthermore, from a Darwinian, evolutionary perspective, Bell (pp. 139–40, 143) makes the point that mismatched marital unions – unions based on 'artificial selection', such as the arrangement between Torquemada and Fidela, which is based on economic interests and social pretension – are shown to be against nature's law and therefore doomed to failure.

43   In *Torquemada en el purgatorio*, the monstrosity of Torquemada's and Fidela's marriage is voiced by Rafael when he says: 'Creí firmemente que el matrimonio absurdo, anti-natural, del ángel y la bestia no tendría sucesión, y ha salido este muñeco híbrido, este monstruo . . .' (*OC*, 1090). Valentín is, according to Rafael, 'un absurdo, un error de la Naturaleza' (*OC*, 1091).

44   William M. Sherzer, 'Death and succession in the *Torquemada* series', *Anales Galdosianos*, XIII (1978), 33–9, 37.

45   Ibid., 36–7.

46   Weber, 27.

47   Ibid.

48   Ibid., 16, 21. Weber, the first critic to discover the existence of these preliminary outlines, has observed that they were found in the same folder as a number of letters written to Galdós by Tolosa Latour. A letter from Tolosa Latour of 1889 suggests that Galdós had sent him the sketches for his perusal and commentary, which has led Weber to suggest that they date from the same year as Tolosa's letter. At the time of writing, the original copy of the preliminary sketches of

Torquemada y San Pedro is missing from the folder where it was originally found in the Casa-Museo Pérez Galdós.

[49] 'Chloro-anaemia' and 'chlorosis' were other terms used in the nineteenth century for 'anaemia'. The disorder owes its name to the greenish-white complexion which characterized the women afflicted by it (the term deriving from the Greek 'chloros', meaning 'green').

[50] See, for instance, Rafael Cervera y Barat, pp. 107–28 (passim); Timoteo Sanz, 'Problemas médico-sociales: Regenerados y degenerados', in *El Siglo Médico*, 39 (14 August 1892), 519. Also, the transactions of the IX Congress of Hygiene and Demography include a number of papers on the issue. In one of these papers (José Fernández y Robina, 'Estadística sobre defunciones por epilepsia', in *Actas del IX Congreso Internacional de Higiene y Demografía*, vol. 12, pp. 308–19), three statistical tables were presented showing the victims of the disease. The first table provides figures of men aged 19 to 21 exempt from the military service due to epilepsy; the second shows the number of epilepsy sufferers in the main Spanish asylums over a number of years; and the third reveals the total deaths from epilepsy in Madrid, also over a period of time. This is illustrative of the anxieties surrounding the disease as a cause of degeneration and death and, more specifically, of the fears about national decline connected with the lower number of military recruits. The second table also reflects the association of epilepsy with mental disease. As with other kinds of degeneration, epilepsy was linked at the time to mental illness and similarly to criminality. Esquerdo, for instance, established a link between epilepsy, moral idiocy (also referred to as 'moral insanity' or 'moral imbecility', a concept indicating a disturbance or total lack of moral sense) and criminality: see J. Esquerdo y Zaragoza, 'Locos que no lo parecen. Garayo "El Sacamantecas"' (1881), in Rey González (ed.), pp. 199–237. The link between epilepsy, criminality and moral insanity was also made by Lombroso, according to whom epileptics showed signs of atavic behaviour (see Peset and Peset, pp. 259–60 and 522–50).

[51] Juan Giné y Partagás, 'El idiotismo', p. 542. Giné continues to say that the adoption of such measure would not be feasible due to the abundance of epileptic individuals, and advises that the matter should be left to private hygiene. Thus he warns: 'evite cada uno, para sí y para los suyos, el entronque con individuos epilépticos o derivados de éstos' (p. 543).

[52] Michelle Perrot (ed.), *A History of Private Life, IV: From the Fires of Revolution to the Great War* (Cambridge, Mass.: Belknap Press of Harvard University Press, 1990), pp. 622–4. As Perrot has observed, women's physiology, and particularly women's fragility, fascinated doctors. During this period, both medical anthologies and fictional works abounded in images of young women with anaemic complexions. There was also a variety of scientific explanations for the disease, which attests to the anxieties it gave rise to.

[53] Hauser ('El siglo XIX', 220) linked *cloro-anemia* with the newly

identified diseases of the nervous system brought about by modern social organization and the pressures of urban life.

54   Manuel Tolosa Latour ('Concepto y fines de la higiene popular', in *Discursos leídos en la Real Academia de Medicina para la recepción pública del académico electo Manuel de Tolosa Latour* [Madrid: Est. Tip. de la viuda e hijos de Tello, 1900], pp. 7–43, 28) refers to a legal measure voted by the American state of Dakota, according to which those suffering from chlorosis (among other kinds of degeneration) would not be permitted to marry. Although Tolosa does not favour the implementation of this measure, promoting instead a hygienic education for marriage, his discussion of it reflects the fears that the spectre of degeneration was generating in medical circles.

55   Weber, 21–2.

56   Torquemada may have suffered here an attack of what Esquirol (vol. 1, p. 117) referred to as 'epilepsia gástrica', which is located in the digestive tract. As Esquirol explains: 'El aparato digestivo puede ser el sitio de la epilepsia; el acceso se presenta cuando hay una irritación gástrica, o cuando se acumulan sustancias indigestas en dicho punto'. It needs to be remembered that Torquemada has difficulties digesting food due to his stomach complaint, and he ends up vomiting the large quantities of food and drink he ingests in Matías Vallejo's tavern.

57   Florencio L. Pérez Bautista (*El tema de la enfermedad en la novela realista española* [Salamanca: Ediciones del Instituto de Historia de la Medicina Española, 1972], pp. 103, 120) notes that anaemia was often regarded in the late nineteenth century as a possible cause of 'neurosis' or nervous diseases. This link had been established, for instance, by Hauser (see n.53).

58   In respect of the critical tendency to emphasize the negative, 'monstrous' nature of Fidela's and Torquemada's marriage and its symbolism, it can be argued that the novels of the series lend themselves to a less negative reading. The text leaves no doubt that Fidela is faithful to Torquemada (her name being reflective of this), in spite of what other characters believe. Also, although Fidela does not love Torquemada, she certainly shows respect and consideration for him, and on one occasion she is seen rebuking Rafael for his lack of respect for her husband. Furthermore, Torquemada is portrayed as a caring husband, who has deep feelings for Fidela. It is also worth noting that Valentín is not described as being totally lacking in feelings: in spite of his fundamental lack of any mental and moral qualities, he is shown to respond positively to the love and attention that his mother gives him. The narrator makes it clear that Valentín begins to deteriorate and to become more animal-like after his mother's death. All of this detracts, to an extent, from the perception of Torquemada's and Fidela's union as essentially 'monstrous'.

59   Fernández Caro, *Los deberes de la sociedad*, p. 11.

60   As noted by Esquirol, vol. 1, p. 121.

61   Campos, Martínez and Huertas (pp. 171–3) have observed that the

diffusion and popularization, via literary works, of medical knowledge and ideas regarding the threat of hereditary degeneration was
common during this period. Significantly, many of these fictional
works were written by medical men. One of them was Giné y
Partagás, who wrote three novels (1884, 1888 and 1890 respectively)
on the issue. The authors of this kind of literature wanted to draw
attention to the threat that parents afflicted by degenerative diseases
posed to the survival of the race. Their texts highlighted the role of
science in laying down the correct codes of behaviour and the
disastrous consequences of disobeying science's mandates.

62   See Manuel Tolosa Latour, *Medicina e higiene de los niños* (Madrid:
Biblioteca Científica Moderna, 1893), p. 159. Tolosa Latour makes a
connection between degenerative diseases and criminality when he
asserts that in those cases in which the degenerate child cannot be
cured 'por ser francamente epiléptico, imbécil e idiota', appropriate
care in asylums should be provided in order to protect society from
their 'terribles impulsos [. . .] borrando de este modo anticipada-
mente la sangre que puede manchar su historia' (p. 160).

63   Manuel Iglesias y Díaz, 'Causas que contribuyen a la mortalidad de
los niños. Medios de remediarlas. Estadísticas comparativas', in *Actas
del IX Congreso Internacional de Higiene y Demografía*, vol. 6, pp. 9–20,
13.

64   Malo, p. 38.

65   Ibid., p. 42. Other hygienists participating in this Congress (including doctors and public health inspectors) expressed similar views,
emphasizing the need to prohibit 'inept' unions in order to prevent
the weakening of the social body through the production of individuals who would never become economically useful: see J. Doncel,
'Causas que contribuyen a la mortalidad de los niños. Medios de
remediarlas. Estadísticas comparativas', in *Actas del IX Congreso Internacional de Higiene y Demografía*, vol. 6, pp. 82–7, 87; and Pedro Laín
Sorrosal, 'Causas que contribuyen a la mortalidad de los niños, y
medio de remediarlas', in *Actas del IX Congreso Internacional de Higiene
y Demografía*, vol. 6, pp. 51–65, 61–2. The danger posed by unhealthy
unions to the future of the race took on greater significance at the
beginning of the twentieth century. Anxieties surrounding this issue
led to a series of debates and proposals regarding the medical
control of marital unions through the intervention of the State,
which culminated in the proposal of a law in 1915 for the 'hygienic
regulation' of marriages. The proponents of these ideas put the
collective defence of society before individual freedom. A doctor
writing for *El Siglo Médico*, for instance, voiced his firm belief that
those suffering from degenerative diseases should restrain from
getting married, on the grounds that 'es preciso sacrificar algo a la
colectividad de nuevas generaciones; de otro modo la sociedad
practica el egoísmo' (see González Alvarez, 585). With reference to
epilepsy in particular, González Alvarez stated, quoting another
author, that 'el celibato se impone al epiléptico' (584). It is highly
ironic, from this perspective, that in the *Torquemada* series Donoso

should advise Torquemada that he remarries in the benefit of the *colectividad*, associating celibacy with selfishness. For a more detailed discussion of the issue of the control of unsuitable unions, see Campos, Martínez and Huertas, pp. 178–93.

66   The control of marriages had first been proposed by George Combe – a famous English phrenologist – in 1835. Combe, who put forward the idea of the hereditary transmission of cerebral, and thus, (positive and negative) mental traits, advised that marriages needed to be regulated in order to improve the race. See Raquel Alvarez Peláez, *Sir Francis Galton, padre de la eugenesia* (Madrid: C.S.I.C., 1985), pp. 60–64.

67   Presidential address to the VII Congress of Hygiene and Demography, 11 August 1891, in *Transactions of the Seventh International Congress of Hygiene and Demography*. London, 10–17 August 1891, ed. by C. E. Shelly. 13 vols (Eyre&Spottiswoode: London, 1892), vol. 10, pp. 7–12.

68   Weber has noted the significance of this comment by Galdós, although he does not focus on the issue of degeneration in connection with a morbid heredity.

69   See, for instance, Cervera y Barat, p. 114. Similarly, Juan Giné y Partagás (*Curso elemental de higiene privada y pública*, 4 vols [Barcelona: Imprenta de Narciso Ramírez y Cñía, 1872], vol. 3, p. 383), asserted that occasional alcoholic intoxication could have an impact on the descendants. Three decades later, Antonio Muñoz Ruiz de Pasanis (*Alcoholismo: su influencia en la degeneración de la raza latina* [Madrid: Ginés Carrión, 1906]) wrote that the 'momento más crítico' for the transmission of an alcoholic inheritance was 'el acto de la concepción', illustrating his thesis with a number of examples from Greek history. Of relevance to the *Torquemada* series is his allusion to a law dictated by Lycurgus – ancient Sparta's renowned lawgiver – which prohibited the spouses from drinking wine on the wedding day (pp. 80–1). It is worthy of note that Muñoz Ruiz de Pasanis's book forms part of Galdós's private collection.

70   Juan Giné y Partagás, *Tratado teórico-práctico de Freno-patología, ó Estudio de las enfermedades mentales fundado en la Clínica y en la fisiología de los centros nerviosos* (Madrid: E. Cuesta, 1876).

71   Cervera y Barat, pp. 114, 115. Morel had already emphasized the constitutional predisposition to cretinism: as observed by Pick, p. 47.

72   Cervera was eager to reveal the conclusions of his study: '[r]esulta [. . .] de las cifras expuestas como hecho culminante que debemos dejar ya consignado, la enorme *disminución en el nivel intelectual de los heredo-alcohólicos*' (p. 109).

73   Cervera y Barat, p. 110.

74   In the same way that alcoholism was believed to be the root of epilepsy, it was also regarded as a main cause of convulsions in childhood, as contemporary doctors, including Tolosa Latour, claimed: see Manuel Tolosa Latour, *Medicina e higiene de los niños*, pp. 155–6; and Esquerdo y Zaragoza, 'Locos que no lo parecen', p. 208. It is noteworthy that in the preliminary version there is no mention of 'rabietas convulsivas' and Galdós simply uses the more

neutral verb 'encolerizarse' with reference to Valentín's violent tantrums. It is also significant that Galdós sent these preliminary outlines to Tolosa Latour for him to comment on the consistency and accuracy of the symptoms, as mentioned in n.48. One can hypothesize that, by portraying Valentín as afflicted by a nervous disorder (manifested in 'rabietas convulsivas'), Galdós is able to reinforce his degenerate state even further without necessarily implying an obvious connection between the son and the father's condition, as he had done in the sketches by describing Valentín as an epileptic.

[75] It is interesting that in this passage Cruz links temperance with respectability when she comments: 'nosotras no lo gastamos [el vino] por mil y quinientas razones, de las cuales con que usted comprenda una sola, basta' (*OC*, 949).

[76] Some critics, like Correa (pp. 140–5), for instance, have emphasized the presentation of the first Valentín as an angel and, in this sense, as a contrast to the monster represented by the second Valentín.

[77] Peset and Peset, pp. 170–97.

[78] As I have argued in *Visions of Filth*, pp. 119–20.

[79] Meningitis is also portrayed as being a result of excessive study by Pardo Bazán, as Pérez Bautista has observed (p. 137).

[80] See Hauser, 'El siglo XIX', 202–24 and 333–58.

[81] Ibid., 343–4.

[82] Ibid., 344.

[83] Fernández Caro, *Los deberes de la sociedad*, p. 32.

[84] The transactions of this Congress include a series of papers on school hygiene (see, for instance, H. Kuborn, 'De l'influence des programmes scolaires sur la santé des enfants', vol. 2, pp. 381–401; and Dr Sikorsky, 'Contribution à l'étude des maladies nerveuses chez les enfants à l'âge scolaire', vol. 2, pp. 453–5, in *Quatrième Congrès international d'hygiène et de démographie à Genève* [du 4 au 9 septembre 1882]). Comptes rendus et mémoires publiés par P.-L. Dunant. 2 tomes, Genève, 1883. See also, in connection with this issue, Menno Huizinga, 'Rapport sur les dangers auxquels est exposé le système nerveux des écoliers et des étudiants par l'application qu'exigent les études et les examens; et sur les moyens d'y remédier', in *Cinquième Congrès international d'hygiène et de démographie* à La Haye, vol. 2, pp. 94–105. Similarly, the International Congress held at Vienna in 1887 devoted a whole section to school hygiene: see *Programme du VI congrès international d'hygiène et de démographie* (du 26 septembre au 2 octobre 1887), Vienne, 1887.

[85] The term *caquexia* refers to a medical condition characterized by extreme and progressive malnutrition caused, among other things, by infections, intoxications and tumors. In *Torquemada en el purgatorio* Rafael uses this word when he declares that his nephew Valentín 'crecerá marcado de cretinismo y de caquexia' (*OC*, 1090).

[86] Malo, p. 41. Another speaker at this Congress stated that '[l]a educación mal dirigida debe colocarse entre las causas de la mortalidad de los niños, y como una de las más poderosas. Las enfermedades del centro nervioso cerebro-espinal, las neurosis y diversos

padecimientos generales pueden ser resultado de una educación viciosa': Manuel Iglesias y Díaz, p. 15. The issue of the pernicious effects of excessive intellectual work and the impact of civilization on children's disease and mortality was also raised by a number of public health experts participating in this Congress (see in particular vol. 5 of the *Actas*).

87 Malo, p. 41.

88 Ricardo Gullón, *Galdós, novelista moderno* (Madrid: Gredos, 1960), pp. 214–18.

89 Aldaraca has made this point in connection with the protagonist of Galdós's *Lo prohibido*, a victim of hysteria. See *El ángel del hogar: Galdós y la ideología de la domesticidad en España* (Madrid: Visor, 1992), p. 166.

90 Aldaraca, pp. 164–5.

91 Dr Velázquez de Castro, 'La responsabilidad en las histéricas', 39, quoted by Aldaraca, p. 165.

92 'La mujer y la política', *La Guirnalda* (20 August 1882), 125–6, quoted by Aldaraca, p. 57. It is worth noting Galdós's links with *La Guirnalda*, a journal in which he published articles and novels. Regarding Galdós's connections with this journal, see Leo Hoar, 'More on the pre- (and post-) history of the *Episodios Nacionales*: Galdós' article "El Dos de mayo" (1874)', *Anales Galdosianos*, VIII (1973), 107–20.

93 According to Charcot, melancholy and depression were one of the main symptoms of male hysteria: as noted by Aldaraca, p. 165.

94 As Showalter has noted (pp. 129–30), hysteria has traditionally been viewed as the quintessential female malady. Hysteria was linked with women in a variety of ways. Its wide array of symptoms – such as fits, fainting, choking, crying, laughing – often occurring in rapid succession, reflected the supposed capriciousness and instability of the feminine nature. Like other aspects of the feminine, hysteria was regarded as elusive and enigmatic, beyond the control of the rationality normally associated with masculinity. In Galdós's novels there are many examples of women who present, at least, some signs of hysteria. Yet, the disorder is not associated exclusively with women – José María Guzmán, the protagonist of *Lo prohibido*, being an obvious example.

95 In fact, one of the books to be found in Galdós's personal library is a medical report by Charcot and A. Hardy (the latter being, like Charcot, a professor at the Faculty of Medicine in Paris) on the issue of the hereditary predisposition to nervous disorders and mental disease. See *Informe de los doctores A. Hardy y J. M. Charcot [. . .] respecto del estado mental de D. Martín Larios y Larios*, Madrid, Est. Tipográfico Sucesores de Rivadeneyra, 1889.

96 Pérez Bautista, pp. 101–05.

97 The term 'neurosis' appeared for the first time in W. Cullen's *Synopsis nosologiae methodicae* (1769) as a synonym for 'nervous disease'. See José María López Piñero, *Los orígenes históricos del concepto de neurosis* (Valencia: Cátedra e Instituto de Historia de la Medicina, 1963), pp. 187–94.

[98] Catherine Jagoe, Alda Blanco and Cristina Enríquez de Salamanca, *La mujer en los discursos de género: Textos y contextos en el siglo XIX* (Barcelona: Icaria, 1998), pp. 339–48, 341–2.

[99] See, for instance, Francisco Javier Santero, *Elementos de higiene privada y pública*, 2 vols (Madrid: El Cosmos, 1885), vol. 2, CXXII; and Jesús Sarabia y Pardo, *El suicidio como enfermedad social* (Madrid: Publicaciones de la Sociedad Española de Higiene, 1889). Suicide had been cited by Morel as one of the kinds of degeneration inherited from the alcoholism of a predecessor, as a contributor to *El Siglo Médico* recorded almost half a century later (see González Alvarez, 584). Contemporary commentators subscribed to this hereditary explanation, although other causes were also acknowledged. Thus, whereas some, like Giné y Partagás (*Tratado teórico-práctico*, p. 455) overemphasized the importance of heredity in creating a predisposition to suicide, others took into consideration social and other causes. Among these was Sarabia y Pardo and A. Brierre de Boismont (*Du suicide et de la folie suicide* [Paris: Librairie Germer Baillière, 1865], pp. 19–20). The latter referred in his study to a large number of psychological and sociological causes of suicide, stating that, although the influence of heredity is 'unquestionable', its role has tended to be exaggerated.

[100] Sherzer, 36.

[101] Antonio Sánchez Barbudo, 'Torquemada y la muerte' *Anales Galdosianos*, II (1967), 45–52. Also, for O'Brien, Rafael represents the decadence of the Spanish aristocracy (118), whereas Peter G. Earle ('Torquemada: hombre-masa', *Anales Galdosianos*, II ([1967], 29–43) writes that: 'El suicidio de Rafael es la protesta del mundo ya caduco de la hidalguía española frente al mundo del voraz progresismo' (39).

[102] Sarabia y Pardo, p. 11.

[103] I have also made this argument in connection with the theme of alcoholism and degeneration in *Angel Guerra*: see *Visions of Filth*, pp. 109–31. In this respect, I find it difficult to agree with Boudreau (H. L. Boudreau, 'The salvation of Torquemada: Determinism and indeterminacy in the later novels of Galdós', *Anales Galdosianos*, XV [1980], 113–28) who, emphasizing Galdós's naturalistic concerns, has argued that the *Torquemada* novels are a 'deterministic study of heredity and environment' (124), comparing the *Torquemada* series to Zola's novels, in which the Macquart blood line produces abnormal types who may be either geniuses or depraved criminals. In relation to the relevance of determinism in Galdós's work, and with specific reference to *La desheredada*, Minter (67–77), although admitting Zola's impact in the novel, has pointed out Galdós's differences with his French contemporary novelist, arguing that Galdós drew mostly on Spanish medical sources, notably on Tolosa Latour and Esquerdo.

Chapter Three

Making a Personal Profit: the Trade of Philanthropy in *Torquemada y San Pedro*

Whereas the previous chapter examined the notion of 'waste versus profit' within *national* and *social* contexts, this chapter addresses it at an *individual* level. The theme of the chapter is philanthropic activity as a 'commercial enterprise', loosely conceived, in which both parties, philanthropist and recipient, intend to benefit materially or spiritually. More specifically, the chapter focuses on the relationship in *Torquemada in San Pedro* (the last novel of the series) between the ex-missionary Gamborena and the 'savage' Torquemada, whom he tries to 'tame' and, as the time of his death approaches, convert to Catholicism (mainly by curing his avarice) so that his soul can be saved.

Although Torquemada's lack of spirituality and his inability to see beyond his own worldly interests has received much critical attention, no detailed study has been produced of the miser's profit-making mentality within the context of the philanthropist–recipient relationship. If we look at Torquemada's obsession with making a profit out of the deal he strikes with Gamborena, which involves Torquemada leaving his riches to the poor in exchange for the salvation of his soul, we see there is one issue that has been overlooked that this chapter explores: the tension that exists between the rational-scientific distribution of charity, and unthinking, wasteful charity. This was a burning issue in contemporary debates on poverty and mendicity. With regard to Gamborena, the other party in the deal, little consideration has been given to his selfishness and business-oriented mentality. It could be argued, indeed, that the ex-missionary is portrayed barely more favourably than the sinner he attempts to reform, whose self-seeking attitude has much more often attracted critical interest. Although some critics, notably Scanlon,[1] have noted Gamborena's business-like approach to religion, this issue has not been analysed in depth nor placed within the context of philanthropy as commercial activity. As I will argue, Gamborena's wish to advise and assist Torquemada hides a less savoury purpose: that of making a 'spiritual' gain out of his conversion. Throughout the novel, and particularly after Torquemada's illness sets in, Galdós puts into question Gamborena's noble and generous instincts, demonstrating that his attempt to save Torquemada's soul is something more than a disinterested philanthropic exercise. The analysis of the relationship between the two parties involved in the deal brings to light parallels between the role of the missionary in non-European, 'uncivilized' countries, and that of the philanthropist working among alien, primitive and 'savage' groups in 'civilized' society, the socio-political role of both missionaries and philanthropists being relevant in this regard. Moreover, a closer analysis of the philanthropist-sinner relationship in respect of the way in which philanthropic control is exercised, particularly at the sinner's death-bed, discloses interesting similarities between Gamborena, the ex-missionary-philanthropist in *Torquemada y San Pedro* and Guillermina Pacheco, his female counterpart in Galdós's previous novel *Fortunata y Jacinta* (1886–7).

In this last novel of the series, Galdós criticizes Gamborena's commercial view of the world, that is to say, his engagement with modern ideas on utility and profit. Further, the author places his critique of utilitarianism within a broader ethical critique of Gamborena's selfish, manipulative and unscrupulous attitudes. As we shall see, Gamborena's relationship with the modern utilitarian discourse is presented as ambiguous, as his traditional ideas on charity distribution show. Although the chapter will concentrate on the last novel of the series, *Torquemada y San Pedro*, some references will be made to *Torquemada en la hoguera* when appropriate.

Gamborena: from Missionary to Philanthropist

The ex-missionary Gamborena, an energetic and ambitious sixty-year-old, who as a young priest used to work as a chaplain in the aristocratic household of the Aguilas, is reunited with Cruz after returning to Spain in his old age. The eldest of the Aguila family, whose admiration and respect for the priest are taken to an exaggerated extent, receives the priest 'como a enviado del Cielo' (*OC*, 1120). Her unwavering faith in Gamborena makes her regard him as the only person who can bring Torquemada under control:

> La verdad, como usted, tan ducho en catequizar salvajes, no eche el lazo a éste y nos le traiga bien sujeto, ¿quién podrá domarle? . . .
> (*OC*, 1118)

That the ex-missionary who has spent most of his life civilizing 'savages' in far-flung countries is now entrusted with the 'taming', or 'civilizing', of Torquemada is significant from the point of view of contemporary ideas linking primitiveness to the lower classes of the population, and both to immorality. It needs to be remembered that although Torquemada has risen to a high social station and his vulgar language and coarse manners have been polished to a great extent by his family – notably by Cruz – he is still perceived as a 'savage' by the upper classes, and his behaviour (his lack of religious feelings, his avarice, his selfishness, cruelty and lack of humanity) viewed as immoral by those around him and also by the narrator, who refers to him as 'salvaje' on several occasions.[2] Torquemada is seen as a 'savage within', a notion which, as we saw in Chapter 2, referred to those marginalized groups of the population at home who were perceived, in the same way as peoples outside Europe, as alien, primitive and a threat to civilized society.[3] Gamborena, who is used to 'la domesticación de las fieras humanas más rebeldes que cabe imaginar' (*OC*, 1184), admits that he finds it harder to 'domesticate' the savages of the civilized world (whom he appropriately calls 'los cafres de la civilización' (*OC*, 1118)) than the uncivilized and barbaric peoples he had to evangelize during his time as a missionary. He says: 'salvajismo por salvajismo, yo prefiero el del otro hemisferio' (*OC*, 1118). This seems to be reflective of contemporary fears of degeneration within the civilized world. Pick has argued that the term *dégénérescence* evolved not only in relation to a 'colonial other' but also in connection with 'primitive' groups at home. As he has stated: 'Evolutionary anthropology functioned not only to differentiate the colonized overseas from the imperial race, but also to scrutinize portions of the population at home: the 'other' was outside and inside'.[4] Social Darwinism and other evolutionary theories in the late nineteenth century, Pick argues, reinforced the imperial discourse of internal unity, although this discourse was constantly haunted by the spectre of degeneration 'within'. Indeed, the dangerous actors of the world of degeneration within 'advanced' societies came to represent more of a threat than the degeneration of those peoples in non-European countries.[5]

Gamborena is the missionary-turned-philanthropist in the civilized world. In fact, it could be said that missionaries and philanthropists played parallel roles, the missionary being the masculine version of the female, home-visiting philanthropist. Nineteenth-century philanthropy was fundamentally an activity connected with middle-class women, its main aim being the moral and religious indoctrination of groups perceived as 'alien' and 'primitive'. Both the missionary and the philanthropist had a controlling – albeit covert, or indirect – socio-political role, whether the danger was at home or outside Europe. In respect of philanthropic enterprise, Donzelot has argued that philanthropy must not be understood as a naively apolitical term: it must be considered as a 'deliberately depoliticizing strategy' whose aim was to serve as an instrument for the indoctrination, surveillance and control of the lower layers of the population with a view to reinforcing social stability.[6] Similarly, religious missions acted as a conduit for European influence. Control by 'main force' in territories that came under imperial domination was often complemented by control in the form of cultural imperialism, including moral-religious indoctrination through missionary endeavour. Further, the construction of the races in the non-European world as physically and mentally inferior, as well as technologically backward, served to legitimize both the West's use of military force and the philanthropic paternalism of the missionary.[7] In a parallel way, the construction in contemporary bourgeois discourses of the lower classes within civilized society as 'immoral' justified the philanthropist's intervention and control.

Both missionaries and philanthropists are portrayed by Galdós in military terms, something that reinforces their political role.

Throughout the account of Gamborena's life, a parallel is drawn between the role of the missionary and that of the soldier. At one point in the narrative, Gamborena reveals his war-like disposition to Cruz, highlighting the similarities between the missionary's works and the skills of warfare:

> Mis compañeros de Congregación dicen [. . .] que cuando Su Divina Majestad dispuso que yo viniese a este mundo, en el momento de lanzarme a la vida estuvo dudando si destinarme a la milicia o a la Iglesia [. . .] En un divino tris estuvo que yo fuese un gran guerrero, debelador de ciudades, conquistador de pueblos y naciones. Salí para misionero, que en cierto modo es oficio semejante al de la guerra y heme aquí que he ganado para mi Dios, con la bandera de la fe, porciones de tierra y de humanidad tan grandes como España. (*OC*, 1119)

Gamborena's exploits in distant territories are made to sound like military exploits. Similarly, his endeavour to convert Torquemada is also turned into a kind of a military *hazaña*. When the ex-missionary first engages in the task of taming Torquemada he thinks to himself: 'Seré su conquistador y le atacaré con cuantas armas hallo en mi arsenal evangélico' (*OC*, 1156). Later on, when Torquemada is approaching his death, Gamborena is seen to engage in a battle against the forces of evil to win the sinner's soul, as we shall see.

There are many traits in Gamborena's character that resemble his feminine counterpart in *Fortunata y Jacinta*, Guillermina. Both Gamborena and Guillermina are described as purposeful, hard-working, persevering and indefatigable. Also, both characters are described as having unflagging energy and a military temperament. We are told that Gamborena did not content himself with being a chaplain in the aristocratic household of the Aguila family, and that his higher aspirations led him to engage in missionary work. As the narrator of *Torquemada y San Pedro* notes: 'Dios le llamaba a mayores empresas que la oscura capellanía de una casa aristocrática' (*OC*, 1120). Gamborena describes himself as a fighter, congratulating himself in his tenacious, strong-willed and adventurous nature:

> Las empresas difíciles son las que a mí me tientan, y me seducen, y me arrastran. ¿Cosas fáciles? Quítate allá. ¡Tengo yo un temperamento militar y guerrero! [. . .] Mi carácter, mi

temperamento, mi ser todo son como de encargo para la lucha, para el trabajo, para las dificultades que parecen insuperables.' (*OC*, 1118–19)

Similarly, the narrator of *Fortunata y Jacinta* points out Guillermina's enterprising and ambitious character: 'La Asociación benéfica a que pertenecía no se acomodaba al ánimo emprendedor de Guillermina, pues quería ella picar más alto, intentando cosas verdaderamente difíciles y tenidas por imposibles.'[8] Like Gamborena, Guillermina has a war-like temperament. The narrator remarks: 'Tenía un carácter inflexible y un tesoro de dotes de mando y de facultades de organización que ya quisieran para sí algunos de los hombres que dirigen los destinos del mundo' (I, 264). Both Guillermina and Gamborena give up their comfortable lives for a life of deprivation in order to achieve their ambitious aims.

In spite of the positive attributes that these two Galdosian characters display, their characterization is clearly double-edged, their favourable traits being offset by their presentation as calculating, self-seeking and domineering. It could be argued that, in *Torquemada y San Pedro*, as in the previous novel *Fortunata y Jacinta*, Galdós's intention was to expose the relationship between the missionary-philanthropist and the sinner as one based on domination and control.[9] In *Torquemada y San Pedro*, the approving, even admiring, depiction of Gamborena is subverted through the use of humour, irony and, on occasions, narrative technique. When the character of the priest is first introduced, the narrator provides an extremely favourable physical description of him (*OC*, 1116–17). After depicting what he calls a 'simpática fisonomía' (*OC*, 1117), the narrator adds a semi-comical note, pointing out that Gamborena's features resembled those of the Buddha. The explanation that the narrator offers is that, as Gamborena spent a good part of his life in the Far East fighting for Christ and against Buddha, the latter, annoyed at the religious persecution, looked the priest in the face for many years, until some of his typical features became projected onto Gamborena's face (*OC*, 1117). A few pages later, after a portrayal of Gamborena's vigorous, enterprising and heroic temperament, which is not devoid of irony, the narrator introduces a less palatable note by calling into question the civilizing role of missionaries:

Dios le llamaba a mayores empresas que la oscura capellanía de una casa aristocrática, y sintiendo en su alma la avidez de los trabajos heroicos, la santa ambición de propagar la fe cristiana, cambiando el regalo por las privaciones, la quietud por el peligro, la salud y la vida misma por la inmortalidad gloriosa, decidió, después de maduro examen, partir a París y afiliarse en cualquiera de las legiones de misioneros con las que nuestra precavida civilización trata de amansar las bárbaras hordas africanas y asiáticas, antes de desenvainar la espada contra ellas. (*OC*, 1120)

The text highlights that the missionary's role was not completely apolitical, thus undermining the narrator's glorifying of the missionary's single-mindedness, courage and determination ('su infatigable ardor de soldado de Cristo' (*OC*, 1120)). The description of Gamborena as a 'soldado de Cristo' is not entirely dictated by the fact that his bravery, fortitude of character and intrepidity liken him to a soldier, but also by the parallel controlling role that both missionaries and the military played in the overseas colonies. The same narrative technique is used in the following paragraph. When the narrator relates Gamborena's fifteen years in Africa, he begins on a highly positive note, drawing attention to the missionary's heroism, vitality and resolution. One could argue, however, that there are resonances of irony in this grand narrative. Also, the admiring presentation of Gamborena is undercut by an allusion at the end of the description to the inflexibility and even aggressiveness that accompanied the missionary's dutiful pursuits:

Quince años estuvo en el Africa tropical trabajando con bravura mística, si así puede decirse; hecho un león de Dios, tomando a juego las inclemencias del clima y las ferocidades humanas; intrépido, incansable, el primero en la batalla, gran catequista, gran geógrafo, explorador de tierras dilatadas, de lagos pestilentes, de abruptas soledades rocosas, desbravando todo lo que encontraba por delante para meter la cruz a empellones, a puñados, como pudiera, en la naturaleza y en las almas de aquellas bárbaras regiones. (*OC*, 1120–1)

In Gamborena's view, any means are legitimate to achieve his end – an end which he regards as honourable. In this respect, his attitude is not dissimilar to Guillermina's, who says to her upper-class friends and relatives: 'No veo más que mi objeto, y me voy derechita a él sin hacer caso de nada' (I, 267).

Gamborena's positive qualities are constantly played down by the narrator, who misses no opportunity to emphasize his imperious and authoritative nature as well as his arrogance and self-contentment.[10] Gamborena certainly does not portray the image of a self-effacing priest. His vanity and exaggerated sense of self are mocked by Galdós in the previously mentioned scene, in which, boasting his military temperament, he says to Cruz that he has won for God 'porciones de tierra y de humanidad tan grandes como España' (*OC*, 1119). Galdós's ridiculing of Gamborena's presumption continues at the beginning of the following chapter. Here, irony can be read in the description of a self-satisfied Gamborena who, fully aware of his ability to hold Cruz in awe, declares bombastically his forthright intention to vanquish Torquemada:

> Aunque la dificultad de este empeño en que la buena de Croisette quiere meterme ahora, me arredra un poquitín—prosiguió, después de dejar, en una pausa, tiempo a la admiración efusiva de la dama—, yo no me acobardo, empuño mi gloriosa bandera y me voy derecho hacia tu salvaje. (*OC*, 1119)

Gamborena's ostentatious attitude and his sense of self-importance are satirized once more during the same conversation with Cruz, when the priest's hand movements designed to silence the spell-bound Cruz are likened to those of an orchestra director:

> [Gamborena] Dio varias vueltas por la estancia, y en una de ellas, sin hacer caso de las exclamaciones exclamativas de su noble interlocutora, se paró ante ella, y le impuso silencio con un movimiento pausado de ambas manos extendidas, movimiento que lo mismo podría ser de predicador que de director de orquesta. (*OC*, 1119)[11]

It is also worth noting the ironic account of the admiration and reverential respect that the two Aguila sisters, and particularly Cruz, have for Gamborena, and their fascination as they listen to Gamborena's exploits as a missionary, which are also described with more than a touch of irony:

> Inútil sería decir que ambas hermanas le tenían por un oráculo y que saboreaban con deleite la miel sustanciosa de sus consejos y doctrina. [. . .]. Cuando, a instancias de las dos señoras, Gamborena se lanzaba a referir los maravillosos episodios de las

misiones de Africa y Oceanía, epopeya cristiana digna de un
Ercilla, ya que no de un Homero que la cantase, quedábanse las
dos embelesadas. (*OC*, 1121)

The irony here is not only directed at the two sisters' capitulation
to Gamborena's seductive power, but also at the priest's vanity and
pomposity, as the reference to his 'hazañas' as an 'epopeya
cristiana digna de un Ercilla, ya que no de un Homero que la
cantase' reveals.

Gamborena reappears in Cruz's life at a time when, after
Rafael's death and the family's move to the Gravelinas palace
(described as 'una entrada en el reino sombrío del aburrimiento
y la discordia' (*OC*, 1120)), she feels particularly vulnerable.
Gamborena becomes a 'tabla de salvación' for Cruz, as the
narrator notes:

Felizmente, Dios misericordioso deparó [. . .] [a Cruz] el consuelo
de un amigo incomparable, que a la amenidad del trato reunía la
maestría apostólica para todo lo concerniente a las cosas
espirituales, un ángel, un alma pura, una conciencia inflexible y un
entendimiento luminoso para el cual no tenían secretos la vida
humana ni el organismo social. Como a enviado del Cielo le
recibió la primogénita del Aguila cuando le vio entrar en su palacio
[. . .] procedente de no sé qué islas [. . .] Se agarró a él como a
tabla de salvación. (*OC*, 1120)

This explains, at least partly, the captivating influence that Gamborena exercises over her and her veneration for the priest,
whose eulogistic portrayal in the above passage cannot be taken at
face value.

The presentation of Gamborena as a warrior goes hand in
hand with his description as a businessman. Gamborena is shown
to engage effectively in business transactions, which adds to the
picture of philanthropic activities as something more than a
simple exercise of altruism and humanitarianism. Gamborena's
business skills are emphasized by the narrator when he reports on
Gamborena's missionary endeavours after being sent to Europe
by his congregation:

Enviáronle después a Europa formando parte de una comisión,
entre religiosa y mercantil, que vino a gestionar un importantísimo
arreglo colonial con el rey de los belgas, y tan sabiamente
desempeñó su cometido diplomático el buen padrito, que allá y

acá se hacían lenguas de la generalidad de sus talentos. "El comercio—decían—le deberá tanto como la fe." (*OC*, 1121)[12]

The inference is that Gamborena is negotiating a business deal. It is ironic that the narrator uses the term 'arreglo colonial' here, as, later in the novel, when Torquemada plans to 'hacer un arreglo' with Gamborena, the priest recriminates him for his use of business terminology (*OC*, 1157). Gamborena's business talents are once more highlighted by the narrator when he observes that at the age of sixty his congregation asked him to return to Europe because 'temían comprometer una vida tan *útil*, exponiéndola a los rigores de aquel bregar continuo con hombres, fieras y tempestades' (*OC*, 1121 [my emphasis]). The use of 'útil' here is significant within the context of the contemporary association between what is useful and what is profitable and productive. Gamborena's congregation capitalizes on the missionary's 'usefulness' and, after his definitive return to Europe, he is entrusted with organizing the 'recaudación de la Propaganda' (*OC*, 1121). Regarding the emphasis on Gamborena's entrepreneurial spirit, it has been noted that religious missions often promoted Western commercial interests.[13] As Gamborena explains to Cruz: '[en] los trabajos de evangelización [. . .] empleábase la diplomacia, la dulzura, el tacto fino o el rigor defensivo, según los casos, ayudando al comercio incipiente o haciéndose ayudar de él' (*OC*, 1122). Gamborena will again use his business skills when he undertakes the task of saving Torquemada's soul. As we shall see, Gamborena turns the miser's conversion into a commercial transaction from which he intends to profit. Leopoldo Alas's observation that in his attempts to convert Torquemada, Gamborena has 'todo el aspecto de un *corredor de número* de los trascedentales negocios ultratelúricos', is pertinent in this respect.[14] Torquemada himself aptly describes Gamborena as '[u]n funcionario de lo espiritual, que viene a prestar servicio cuando le llaman' (*OC*, 1162). It is ironic, therefore, that when Torquemada asks Gamborena for guarantees that the afterlife exists, the missionary, enraged, should say to him: '¿Soy acaso algún corredor o agente de Bolsa?' (*OC*, 1157).

The exchange in which Gamborena and Torquemada become involved in attempting to save the latter's soul is certainly not the typical, traditional relationship between a middle-class female philanthropist and a recipient from the lower classes. In spite of the fact that in *Torquemada y San Pedro* we are presented with a male philanthropist, and a recipient who has risen from the lower layers of society to the ranks of the aristocracy, it could be argued that this relationship has many elements in common with that of the middle-class female philanthropist and the lower-class recipient. As we have seen, the missionary can be regarded as playing a similar role to that of the female philanthropist in the 'civilized' world. Also, although Torquemada is now, in theory, a member of the upper classes, in Gamborena's eyes he is still part of the 'savage', uncivilized and morally inferior lower classes.[15] It is ironic therefore that Gamborena should say to Torquemada, when he begins his indoctrination programme, that when it comes to the teaching of the doctrine he has no regard for social position, in this particular case Torquemada's high social station: 'no hago caso de jerarquías, ni de respetabilidades, sean las que fueren. No extrañe pues, mi señor don Francisco, que en el asunto que aquí nos reúne le trate como a un chiquillo de escuela' (*OC*, 1153). The reason why Gamborena can afford to treat the now 'respectable' Torquemada in a patronizing and condescending way is that he is fully conscious of his moral superiority and this justifies, in his eyes, the control he attempts to exert over him. That Gamborena is higher up in the moral hierarchy is emphasized by the priest himself when he tells Torquemada, in a self-assured tone: 'usted frente a mí, *mediando el caso moral que media*, no es el señor marqués, ni el millonario, ni el respetabilísimo senador, sino un cualquiera, un pecadorcillo, sin nombre ni categoría, que necesita de mi enseñanza' (*OC*, 1153–4 [my emphasis]). Torquemada may have climbed the social ladder and become a *marqués* and a *senador* through his union with the (ruined) aristocracy and through the new contacts that his social ascent has provided, but the fact is that Gamborena views him, essentially, as an immoral miser from a working-class background.[16]

In *Torquemada y San Pedro*, in spite of Torquemada's social station, the moral barrier between him and the philanthropist, as well as other members of the upper classes, is obvious.[17] Gamborena humiliates and degrades Torquemada in a scene in which, after rebuking him for his animosity towards Cruz, he tells him that the reason for his hostility and hatred is that he feels morally and intellectually inferior to her:

En ella todo es grande, en usted todo es pequeño, y su habilidad
para ganar dinero, arte secundario y de menudencias, se siente
humillada ante la grandeza de los pensamientos de Cruz. Es usted
[. . .] en esta industria de los negocios el simple obrero que
ejecuta, ella la cabeza superior que concibe planes admirables. Sin
Cruz no sería usted más que un desdichado prestamista, que se
pasaría la vida amasando un menguado capital con la sangre del
pobre. Con ella lo ha sido todo y se ha empingorotado a las alturas
sociales. (*OC*, 1154)

Donzelot has observed that one characteristic of nineteenth-
century philanthropy that distinguished it from older forms of
charity was that the new system of philanthropy used less obvious
instruments of control, notably moral advice and exhortation, as
opposed to humiliating charity and repression. The philanthropic
strategy involved 'positive power' rather than 'destructive repression'.[18] It was believed that moral advice had to be given in a
subtle way, that is, the philanthropist had to be seen not as
exercising control but 'legitimate moral influence' over the
recipient.[19] As the main aim of nineteenth-century philanthropy
was to improve or reform the character of those controlled, this
necessarily implied the existence of a moral code of behaviour
which placed the philanthropist higher in the hierarchy than the
recipient. Thus, in spite of the image of benevolence and humanitarianism that the new system of philanthropy was trying to
convey, the philanthropists' awareness of their moral superiority
made it in practice very difficult to maintain a balance between
the authoritarian, disciplinary and patronizing approach on the
one hand, and the humanitarian and altruistic approach on the
other.[20] The desire to establish a one-to-one disinterested relationship often deteriorated into a control-dependency relationship,
which inevitably led to an amount of interference and intrusive-
ness on the part of the philanthropist. This in turn often generated resentment, mistrust and rebellious reactions among those
whom philanthropists were trying to reform, which deflected the
philanthropist's controlling aim. If the recipient accepted will-
ingly the philanthropist's interference, it has been argued, it was
because they thought they could obtain a gain in exchange.[21] The
relationship between Gamborena and Torquemada is illustrative,
in many ways, of how this new philanthropic strategy worked.

Wasteful Charity? Ensuring a Fair Deal with Gamborena

In the first scene in which Gamborena and Torquemada are seen interacting, we find out that Torquemada has been unable to sleep because of a *sermón* that Gamborena had given him the previous night (*OC*, 1116). Later on, the narrator stresses Torquemada's fear of Gamborena and the mistrust he inspires him, pointing out that: '[Gamborena] siempre acababa echándole sermones que le ponían triste, y llenaban su espíritu de zozobra y recelo' (*OC*, 1153). On one occasion in which the missionary approaches Torquemada to urge him to reconcile himself with his sister-in-law, Cruz, it is clear that Torquemada does not welcome his interference. Thus, irritated by Gamborena's lengthy introduction to the matter he intended to raise, Torquemada thinks to himself: 'A ver por dónde sale este tío', and says to Gamborena, 'con cierta displicencia': 'Bueno, señor mío, diga pronto lo que . . .' (*OC*, 1154).[22] Torquemada has a hostile attitude towards Gamborena and reluctantly accepts his *sermones* and his philanthropic paternalism. Though later on he seems more favourable and receptive to the priest's intervention, it is only because he thinks that he can profit from it. Thus, after submitting his will to Gamborena ('aquí me tiene dispuesto a obedecerlo en cuanto quiera mandarme', Torquemada tells him) he talks about making a deal with him (*OC*, 1157). In spite of Torquemada's assertion that he is willing to obey the priest in everything he advises, it becomes obvious that he expects to gain a benefit in exchange.[23] Gamborena's advice to Torquemada is that in order to save his soul he must not forget to be generous to the poor in his will. Torquemada's decision to give his riches away is subject to the deal he hopes to strike with Gamborena, which entails the priest securing the miser's entrance to heaven in exchange for his charity. As Galdós clearly shows, Torquemada regards the poor as wasteful, his views on charity and its distribution being reflective of those of contemporary writers on the issue. However, he is willing to part with his money so long as he can exact a profit, or, put in other words, so long as the transaction does not represent a wasted opportunity for him.

Charity in the *Torquemada* novels has tended to be examined as a Christian value, generally from the perspective of Torquemada's lack of spirituality and humanity, and his inability to perform charitable acts. Within the broader analysis of the idea of waste versus profit, it can be stated that Galdós was also concerned with the social implications of charity distribution, and particularly with the indiscriminate allocation of charitable funds, a burning question at the time, present in the writings of philanthropists, public health experts and other social and moral observers. By raising the issue of charity-giving and Torquemada's position regarding the matter, Galdós was not merely drawing attention to Torquemada's spiritual deficiencies, but echoing contemporary social concerns.

Contemporary views on charity stemmed from the transformations brought about by the processes of industrialization and urbanization. Against a backdrop of abrupt social and economic change and the arrival of a virulent market-led political economy, the Church was forced to adapt its ideology to the new circumstances. The long-standing notion of the destitute as 'Christ's poor ones', as innocent victims of the lot that life had bestowed upon them, was gradually replaced by a view of the poor which associated them with ideological and, potentially, violent protest – protest that sought a radical re-arrangement of the existing order. Attitudes to poverty underwent an important change. The providential origin of poverty began to be questioned, as did the traditional deferential image of the poor as 'unfortunates' who were justifiably dependent on the charity of the rich. Poverty came to be seen as arising from dissolute and immoral behaviour, self-inflicted by those who eschewed self-help. Based on its indiscriminate nature, the argument was made by the religious establishment, as well as by political economists, government officials and social commentators, that the giving of alms to beggars was useless and wasteful, and merely encouraged further immorality and indolence.

The sense that the wealthier classes had a moral obligation to help the poor fell away. Writers on social and moral issues, as well as dispensers of charity, increasingly felt that a discrimination in the distribution of charity was required. It was observed that the poor were poor for different reasons, and so they had to be dealt with in different ways. The crux of the changing attitude to poverty, something which was not exclusive to Spain, was the classification of the poor into two broad categories: the 'deserving' and the 'undeserving'. The deserving poor displayed, or desired to embrace, 'respectable' values: perseverance, punctuality, thrift, temperance, self-improvement, cleanliness, hard work, and so on. Such poor people had fallen on hard times due to circumstances beyond their control, unlike the undeserving poor, whose impoverishment was deemed self-inflicted, arising from their dissolute, unhygienic and wasteful lifestyles, and innate propensity for 'vices'. Charity given indiscriminately to this category of poor was believed to lead to moral degradation.

These changing attitudes to poverty and charity-giving were driven to a large degree by economic considerations: the undeserving poor were non-productive and of no use, materially, to society. Moreover, they were also seen not just as a social burden but also as a drain on economic resources and a drag on economic growth. Indiscriminate charity came to be regarded as harmful to the economic and political interests of the nation; thus it became closely associated with waste, and was seen to initiate a vicious circle that led to immorality and, in turn, a further waste of material resources. Constancio Bernaldo de Quirós and José M. Llanas Aguilaneido, quoting Concepción Arenal, stated in this regard that, if in the old days charity was essentially 'pathological', nowadays it should be 'hygienic', that is, beneficial, or profitable, both to the recipient and to society.[24]

In asking Torquemada to succour the poor, Gamborena does not discriminate between the different kinds of poor, holding on to traditional beliefs. It is important to note in this respect that Gamborena's ideological stance is shown to be inconsistent by Galdós. Gamborena's conversion of philanthropy into a commercial exercise based on fair exchange – in the same way as his engagement earlier in his life with a commercially motivated imperialist project – is illustrative of his complicity with a utilitarian and mercantile view of the world. But although in *Torquemada y San Pedro* he is shown to consciously subscribe to modern utilitarian notions, in other respects his ideas are in keeping with the views of the traditional Catholic Church prior to the mid nineteenth century. His traditional beliefs on charity and the poor are an obvious example of this. Gamborena's conservative views on charity are illustrative of the fact that the emergence of new attitudes towards charity and poverty was still a slow process and that the old conception of the poor as receptacles of the charity of the wealthier classes – and similarly as an instrument for the rich to ensure their entry to heaven – still survived in the nineteenth century.[25] There is one humorous passage in the novel in which Torquemada voices traditional ideas on poverty in a slightly mocking way. When Gamborena advises him that in order to 'purify' his soul he should leave his money to the poor, Torquemada replies: 'Pero ¿no dicen ustedes que es muy bonito ser pobre? Dejadlos, dejadlos y no nos metamos a quitarles su divina miseria' (*OC*, 1178). Torquemada's words reflect the old belief, based on primitive Christianity, that associated poverty with sanctity. These views, according to which the poor were an object of special predilection of divine providence, and their lot in this world was a means of gaining access to the riches of the afterlife, were a powerful instrument of social stability at a time when social tensions had begun to increase. The continual preaching of 'resignation' to the poor was a means of slowing working-class social mobility, while encouraging it in the middle classes. With the development of capitalism, particularly after its full onset, the possibility of social mobility undermined old beliefs which attributed one's position in life to providence. Torquemada's suggestion to Gamborena that the poor should remain poor and should not be taken out of their saintly state smacks of the author's mockery of old perceptions of the destitute as 'Christ's poor ones'. As we saw in Chapter 1, Galdós disapproved of self-enforced poverty and the passive acceptance of one's lot in life, an attitude which disregarded material, civilizing progress. He also condemned, however, a materialistic and rationalistic approach totally devoid of the spiritual element, precisely the approach taken by Torquemada. In fact, the passage discussed above can also be read as the author's criticism of Torquemada's materialism and his egoistic motives: clearly, the ancient belief which associated poverty with sanctity did not imply in any way the suppression of charity, as Torquemada suggests: indeed, charity acted as a vehicle for social order and stability.

In *Torquemada en la hoguera* and *Torquemada y San Pedro*, the protagonist is shown to subscribe to the more rational and scientific attitudes towards charity that had began to emerge in the second half of the nineteenth century. It becomes obvious that the motives for his giving are self-interested: he is only willing to assist the poor because he fears that if he is not charitable he will not be able to save his soul. After his first conversation with Gamborena – in which the priest rebukes him for his hatred towards Cruz and finally causes fear and alarm in Torquemada by 'listing' his moral shortcomings (*OC*, 1156) – Torquemada, aware that his death may be close and under Gamborena's pressure, decides to find a 'solution' to the problem: 'yo acepto cualquier solución que usted formule. [. . .] ¿Hay que dar algo a los necesitados? Pues no hay inconveniente. Conque . . ., ya tiene usted a su salvaje convertido' (*OC*, 1156). It becomes clear from this quotation that Torquemada's charity is self-seeking and that he can only conceive his salvation as a business. As he explains to Gamborena, his 'objetivo' is '*ganar* el cielo' (*OC*, 1156 [my emphasis]), and he continues to say: 'Ganarlo digo, y sé muy bien lo que significa la *especie*' (*OC*, 1156 [my emphasis]), hence equating spiritual and material gain. But in order to 'ganar el cielo' Torquemada will need to become *deserving of* it. In a world dominated by the exchange mentality, nothing is given for free. Thus, when confused about why he cannot be saved he asks the priest, '¿qué he hecho yo para no salvarme?' (*OC*, 1156), Gamborena replies that the question that he should be asking himself is: '¿Qué hago yo para *merecer* mi salvación?' (*OC*, 1156 [my emphasis]), and shortly afterwards he warns the miser: 'Ni yo soy el portero celestial [. . .] ni aunque lo fuera abriría la puerta para quien no *mereciese* entrar' (*OC*, 1158 [my emphasis]). The stress placed on the idea of *merecer* is important here. In a previous sequence, when Gamborena is having a conversation with Fidela and Augusta about the issue of the Final Judgement, Gamborena tells the women that confiding in the 'divina misericordia' is not sufficient to gain access to heaven: one needs to prove that one is deserving of something in order to receive it (*OC*, 1134). It is not surprising, therefore, that when Gamborena urges Torquemada to give his immense riches to the poor in order to make himself deserving of salvation, Torquemada should have resource to the same 'exchange' ethic: he asks himself if the poor are really deserving of his charity or if his money will be wasted. Torquemada believes that the discriminatory criterion must be applied to everyone: if God discriminates between those who deserve entry to heaven and those who do not, by the same logic, he should be discriminating in his charity giving.

The issue of the deserving and undeserving poor and the unthoughtful distribution of charity was raised by Galdós in other novels written in the 1890s – notably *Angel Guerra*, *Nazarín*, *Halma* and *Misericordia*. In these novels, Galdós highlights the difficulty of differentiating between those poor who are deserving of charity and those who are not, although he does not attempt to provide an answer to the problem. The ambiguity surrounding the issue of deserving and undeserving poverty (particularly in *Nazarín*) prevents the reader from reaching a definitive conclusion regarding how charitable funds should be administered. In *Torquemada en la hoguera* and *Torquemada y San Pedro*, the question of charity distribution is once more problematized without any attempt to offer a solution.

Torquemada's rational views are contrasted to the traditional beliefs upheld by the ex-missionary-philanthropist. Galdós, by distancing himself from his protagonist in the first and last novel of the series – and also from Gamborena in *Torquemada y San Pedro* – refuses once more to make his views explicit. In keeping with his utilitarian principles, Torquemada is only willing to give in return for a perceived benefit. Thus he says to the priest: 'Francisco Torquemada está dispuesto a dejarse gobernar por el padre Gamborena, como el último de los párvulos, siempre que el padre Gamborena le garantice . . .' (*OC*, 1157). It is the same give-and-take mentality which governed his actions and thoughts in *Torquemada en la hoguera*, and which prevented him from comprehending why God did not save his son Valentín in spite of his 'over-generosity' with the poor. The idea of giving for the sake of it, without receiving some kind of payment in exchange, is beyond his understanding because it is wasteful. Thus, he continues to badger the priest:

> Pero usted me ha de garantizar que, una vez en su poder mi conciencia toda, se me han de abrir las puertas de la Gloria eterna, que ha de franqueármelas usted mismo, puesto que llaves tiene para ello. Haya por ambas partes lealtad y buena fe, ¡cuidado!, porque, francamente, sería muy triste, señor misionero de mis entretelas, que yo diera mi capital y que luego resultara que no había tales puertas, ni tal gloria, ni Cristo que los fundó . . . (*OC*, 1157)

As Torquemada engages in a business transaction with Gamborena he needs to ensure that the arrangement will benefit both sides, and that both sides involved will show loyalty and good will. Torquemada needs to have the certainty that he is embarking on a *fair* deal, by which he understands one that will be profitable. Of relevance here is the utilitarian association, as discussed in Chapter 1, between what is just and what is profitable. It should be noted that in spite of Torquemada's materialistic and selfish attitude in the previous passage, the humour surrounding his over-rational approach to his salvation – his desperate attempts at securing a *bona fide* deal – detracts from the perception of the miser in a completely negative light.

That Torquemada is 'trading' with Gamborena is highlighted by the language used both by Torquemada and by the narrator throughout this episode. One obvious example of this is the passage in which he asks Gamborena to explain what he needs to do in order to 'obtain' the salvation of his soul:

> ¿Qué tengo que hacer para salvarme? Explíquese pronto y con la claridad que debe emplearse en los negocios. Yo [. . .] quiero y necesito la salvación. Hasta por mi decoro debo solicitarla. [. . .] ahora dígame qué tengo que *hacer* o qué tengo que *dar* para *obtener ese resultado.* (*OC*, 1178)

It is noteworthy that Torquemada talks about 'solicitar' his salvation, as if it were a loan. Also, the use of 'dar' and 'obtener ese resultado' reinforce Torquemada's give-and-take mentality. After attempting to make a contract with Gamborena, Torquemada calculates that the chances of being saved depend on his being charitable to the poor, and agrees to leave his money to 'repartir socorros'. However, as a good utilitarian, he says to Gamborena: 'aunque, la verdad, nunca me ha gustado *dar pábulo* a la holgazanería' (*OC*, 1178). Here, Torquemada is linking mendicity and unthinking alms-giving with idleness and immorality, in keeping with ideas expressed by contemporary commentators, who propounded the ethic of work and warned that an unthoughtful distribution of charity fostered inactivity and led to moral debasement.[26] The association of indiscriminate charity and lack of morals is established again by Torquemada in a passage in which he asks Cruz what she thinks about Gamborena's suggestion that a large portion of his money should go to the poor:

> ¿Usted qué opina? ¿Debo dejar mucho para los pobres? ¿En qué forma, en qué condiciones? No olvide usted que a veces todo lo que se les da va a parar a las tabernas, y si se les da ropa, va a parar a las casas de empeño. (*OC*, 1181)

By asking how his money should be distributed ('¿En qué forma, en qué condiciones?'), Torquemada is making the point that he does not want his *capital* wasted on the undeserving poor. Torquemada's ideas on charity are the same as those that motivated his behaviour in *Torquemada en la hoguera*, when he attempted to buy his son's life in return for his charity to the poor. In this first novel, there is also clear evidence that, in Torquemada's view, the poor are wasteful, and he only gives in order to obtain a tangible benefit: Valentín's life. Thus, when tía Roma advises him to sell a pearl he possesses and give the money to the poor, he replies: 'Seguiré tu consejo, aunque, si he de ser franco, eso de dar a los pobres viene a ser una tontería, porque cuanto les das se lo gastan en aguardiente' (*OC*, 931). After Valentín's death, feeling that God has not kept his word, Torquemada goes back on his intention of succouring the poor, associating them with improvidence:

> Total, que lo que pensaba emplear en favorecer a cuatro pillos . . ., ¡mal empleado dinero, que había de ir a parar a las tabernas, a los garitos y a las casas de empeño! . . ., digo que esos dinerales los voy a gastar en hacerle a mi hijo del alma [. . .] el entierro más lucido que en Madrid se ha visto (*OC*, 935).

Torquemada once more voices contemporary bourgeois discourses which regarded poverty as self-inflicted and the poor as intrinsically immoral and dissolute.[27]

Although Torquemada has very clear views on charity and its distribution, in *Torquemada y San Pedro* these views change in accordance with the ebb and flow of his illness. This is illustrated in a significant passage when there is a relapse in his illness and he asks Gamborena to return his 'cape', that is, the money he was intending to give to the poor.[28] It should be remembered, in this respect, that when the first Valentín was ill, Torquemada had given a beggar his *old* cape in the hope that God would spare his son's life. In *Torquemada y San Pedro*, Torquemada tells Gamborena about his physical resemblance with that beggar. This prompts the missionary to ask the miserly Torquemada for his *new* cape, implying, through this metaphor, that he needs to give the poor all that he can as opposed to the 'leftovers' (*OC*, 1179–80). Torquemada, in the belief that giving away his 'new cape' may not bring him anything in return, decides not to waste his money on the poor, whom he once more associates with idleness and dissolution. He tells the priest: 'Y mi capa, ¿dónde está? Bien puede devolvérmela . . . La necesito, tengo frío y no he trabajado yo toda la vida para el obispo ni para que cuatro holgazanes se abriguen con mi paño' (*OC*, 1190). Torquemada finally decides to change his will in favour of Valentín, leaving all his money to him (the only 'decent' person around him, as he considers that his mental incapacity renders him harmless), reserving just a small amount for the poor. Torquemada, continuing with the metaphor, offers cast-offs once more, as he did when he gave his old cape to the beggar in *Torquemada en la hoguera*. Thus he informs Gamborena: 'en cuanto a la capa [. . .] le digo a usted que vuelve a mi poder, sin que esto quiera decir que yo dé algo, una cosa prudencial, verbigracia, un chaleco en buen uso' (*OC*, 1191).

Throughout this episode, the protagonist's obsession with ensuring a gain in exchange for his charitable actions is emphasized. On one occasion he asks Gamborena: 'Y ¿con buenas acciones tengo segura la . . .?' (*OC*, 1179). Similarly, when Cruz advises him to give a third of his fortune entirely to the poor (the other two-thirds would be shared equally between his two children), he exclaims: '¡Todo! . . . a la Iglesia . . . [. . .] Y de este modo me aseguran que . . .?' (*OC*, 1182). Finally, Torquemada accedes to giving a third of his *legítima* to the Church because he can see the benefits he can obtain from it. He has not changed his mind about his ideas on the distribution of charity: '¡Todo a la Iglesia! . . . Bueno, Señor, me contento con tal que me salve' (*OC*, 1182). As long as he knows that his place in heaven is guaranteed, he does not mind aiding the poor, in spite of his utilitarian ideas regarding the indiscriminate distribution of charity. Whether the poor are deserving or undeserving of his money becomes less important than the fact that his charity can make him 'deserving' of salvation. Thus, he is dismayed to hear from Gamborena that giving is not sufficient unless it is accompanied by a genuine feeling of charity: 'Ahora, ahora, después del sacrificio que acabo de hacer . . ., ¡todo, Señor, todo! . . ., ahora ¿no *merezco* yo que se me diga, que se me asegure . . .?' (*OC*, 1183 [my emphasis]). After Torquemada makes the decision to surrender his money to the poor, he constantly needs reassurance that he will be saved in return.

There is one interesting passage in the last novel which clearly illustrates Torquemada's fear that Gamborena may 'break the deal'. In this passage, Torquemada is shown to react with surprise on finding out that Gamborena is not interested in making any material profit out of his death. Neither is he expecting to take control of the distribution of the money. As the priest explains:

Al pedir a usted la capa le signifiqué que no olvidara en sus disposiciones a los menesterosos, a los hambrientos, a los desnudos. Nunca pensé que mi petición se interpretara como un propósito, como un deseo de que la capa, o el valor de la capa, viniese a mis manos, para rasgarla y distribuir sus pedazos. Estas manos no tocaron jamás dinero de nadie, ni han recibido de ningún moribundo manda ni legado. Delo usted a quien quiera. (*OC*, 1183)

Gamborena also adds that his congregation does not accept 'donativos testamentarios', as they live on alms. Torquemada, disheartened, says to the priest: '¿De modo que . . . no quiere . . .? Pues yo accedí, pensando en usted, en su congregación, que es toda de santos [. . .] Pero usted no me abandonará. Usted me dirá que me salvo' (*OC*, 1183). The inference of Torquemada's words is that if Gamborena is not going to draw a material benefit, there is no reason why he should feel obliged to secure his salvation and he may therefore lose interest in the deal and 'abandon' him. Of course, what Torquemada does not realize is that although Gamborena does not intend to draw any material benefit, he is intent on making a spiritual profit out of the business of saving his soul, something which is evident from the beginning of Gamborena's indoctrinating mission. Although Gamborena scolds Torquemada for his use of business language and his intention to 'hacer un arreglo' with him ('no admito bromas en este terreno, y para que nos entendamos olvide usted las mañas, los hábitos y hasta el lenguaje de los negocios' (*OC*, 1157)), a few lines earlier the priest was shown using business-related terminology when he warns Torquemada that he cannot guarantee his eternal salvation and that '[e]l negociante que dude de la seguridad de ese Banco en que deposite sus capitales, ya se las entenderá luego con el demonio . . .' (*OC*, 1157).[29] Galdós makes abundantly clear in the series that the priest's attempt to save Torquemada's soul is itself a commercial transaction: Gamborena does not want to invest 'spiritual capital' in converting Torquemada without getting anything in return.[30]

On Torquemada's Death-bed: the Philanthropist's Struggle for Control

The exchange deal between Torquemada and Gamborena, a deal from which both parties attempt to benefit, is reflective of the raw mentality of profit and gain of the period. The priest fits into the utilitarian ethic of gain versus waste as much as Torquemada. In fact, there is not much difference between Torquemada's charity and Gamborena's philanthropy: Gamborena is as business-oriented, self-interested and manipulative as the sinner he is trying to reform. Like Torquemada, Gamborena does not want to waste the chance of gaining access to heaven. At one point in the novel, when Gamborena realizes that Torquemada is not responding to his indoctrination, the narrator comments: '[Gamborena] veía con desconsuelo el giro que iba tomando *el negocio de aquella conciencia,* y cuán expuesto era *perder la partida* si la infinita misericordia no abría caminos nuevos por donde menos se pensara' (*OC*, 1162 [my emphasis]). Here, the idea of wasting the opportunity of making a profit out of Torquemada's soul is emphasized. The portrayal of Gamborena as enterprising, energetic, persevering and determined fits the image of the self-made man,[31] albeit one who embarks on 'negocios ultratelúricos', as Leopoldo Alas put it. Prochaska has noted the links between capitalism and charitable 'enterprise'.[32] He has commented, within the British context, that the stress laid by British Protestants on individualism as the basis for spiritual progress corresponded with the *laissez-faire* ethos of the secular world, where individual energy and initiative were seen to lead to material success. The same argument could be made in connection with philanthropic enterprises in Spain, as Protestant and Catholic notions of philanthropy became very close after the rise of industrial capitalism.

Gamborena is shown by Galdós to take advantage of the favourable circumstances offered by Torquemada's illness and the proximity of his death for his own interested purposes. Galdós is intent on demonstrating, once more, that philanthropic activities were not merely inspired by benevolence, selflessness and good-will, and that philanthropists were often also spurred by a desire for control and domination. This is not the first time that Galdós portrays in his fiction the interaction between philanthropist and recipient in the vital period leading to the sinner's death in order to expose the shortcomings of philanthropic enterprise. Indeed, the episode of Torquemada's illness and death bears numerous similarities to the account of Mauricia *la dura*'s last few days in *Fortunata y Jacinta*.[33] Both Mauricia and Torquemada are perceived as ungovernable and rebellious, and both are similarly described as 'savages'. With the proximity of death, both characters become more docile, compliant and easily influenced, which provides the philanthropist/missionary with an ideal opportunity to intervene, because control can be exerted with less constraint.[34] But gaining control over the penitent is shown to be a challenging task in both novels. Throughout the episode of their illness and death, both Mauricia and Torquemada oscillate between compliance with the philanthropist/missionary's requests and rebelliousness. If the genuineness of Mauricia's repentance is undermined by the fact that it is often presented as a result of the coercion exercised by the philanthropist and fear of punishment, in *Torquemada y San Pedro* the author demonstrates that Torquemada's submissiveness and obedience are also triggered by fear and external pressure. In this respect, Prochaska has shown that the instillation of a sense of guilt and shame in the sinner was used as a major instrument of indoctrination and control.[35] In this way, the philanthropist could win the recipient's humility, which would in turn prepare the ground for repentance and reformation.[36] In *Torquemada y San Pedro* there is a humorous passage in which Torquemada tells Gamborena that he has no sins to confess. Here, the humour plays down not only Torquemada's sins but also the significance of Gamborena's indoctrinating mission:

> Aunque usted se enoje, señor Gamborena de mis pecados . . ., de mis pecados no, porque no los tengo . . . Señor Gamborena de mis virtudes . . ., aunque usted se escandalice, tengo que decirle que soy un santo. (*OC*, 1177)

In order not to suffer defeat Gamborena will try to instil fear in his victim by mentioning the torments of hell, something which achieves the desired controlling effect, as Torquemada's reaction shows: 'Bah! . . . Ya viene usted de malas—dijo Torquemada con fingido humor de bromas y completamente acobardado—' (*OC*, 1178). In spite of Cruz's assertion that Torquemada regards Gamborena as a superior being, 'un ángel o un apóstol' (*OC*, 1119), there is evidence to argue that Torquemada's attitude towards Gamborena is also inspired by fear and not merely by respect. In an early scene in the novel, the missionary himself comments that Torquemada may be fearful of him. In this scene, the narrator draws attention to Gamborena's self-congratulatory attitude regarding the impact of his indoctrination on Torquemada. The priest seems absolutely certain – in a rather conceited and self-satisfied way – that the sinner will fall under his powerful evangelical spell. As he says to Cruz:

> Temor o respeto, ello es que se impresiona con las verdades que me oye. Y no le digo más que la verdad, la verdad monda y lironda, con toda la dureza intransigente que me impone mi misión evangélica. Yo no transijo; desprecio las componendas elásticas en cuanto se refiere a la moral católica. Ataco el mal con brío, desplegando contra él todos los rigores de la doctrina. El señor Torquemada me ha de oír muy buenas cosas, y temblará y mirará para dentro de sí [. . .] Déjale, déjale de mi cuenta. (*OC*, 1119)

As this quotation reveals, fear of the strictures of the Catholic doctrine acts as an effective instrument of control.

Fear of punishment will intensify as the seriousness of Torquemada's condition becomes a reality. The obvious deterioration of his heath after his eating and drinking binge at Matías' tavern is an important point in the process of his illness and has a profound effect on Torquemada's state of mind. When he recovers consciousness after his 'attack of indigestion' the author shows that the outward manifestation of his feelings of tenderness and affection, not only towards his daughter Rufinita but also towards Cruz, Donoso and Gamborena, are to a large extent a product of his fear of death, as well as of his weak physical and emotional state. The role played by genuine contrition is dubious:[37]

> En su resurrección [. . .] salió el pobre don Francisco por el registro patético y de la ternura, que tan bien armonizaba con su debilidad física y con el desmayo de sus facultades. Dio en la flor de pedir perdón a todo quisque, de emocionarse por la menor cosa, y de expresar vehementes afectos a cuantas personas se acercaban a su lecho para consolarle. [. . .] Al través de todas estas manifestaciones sentimentales, advertíase en el ánimo del enfermo un miedo intensísimo. (*OC*, 1174)

This passage bears close resemblance to the scene in *Fortunata y Jacinta* in which Mauricia's apparent repentance is similarly presented as mainly motivated by the proximity of death. As doña Lupe relates:

> La infeliz tarasca viciosa, con [. . .] las ternezas de Doña Guillermina, y más aún, con la proximidad de la muerte, estaba que parecía otra, curada de sus maldades y arrepentida *en toda la extensión de la palabra*, diciendo que se quería morir lo más católicamente posible, y pidiendo perdón a todos con unos ayes y una religiosidad tan fervientes que partían el corazón. (II, 171)

Torquemada's intense fear is highlighted once more some time after, when he suffers a relapse in his illness and is advised to have the sacraments administered. The narrator describes eloquently the effect that this has on the moribund Torquemada:

> don Francisco [. . .] se había quedado sin aliento y sintió un frío mortal que hasta los huesos le penetraba. Por un instante creyó que el techo se le caía encima como una losa y que la estancia se quedaba en profunda oscuridad. Su inmenso pánico le dejó sin palabra y hasta sin ideas. (*OC*, 1180)

Here, as in the episode when he was taken home seriously ill from Matías's tavern, Torquemada's mildness of character, his humility, passivity and complete lack of will, are shown to be prompted by his impending death:

> La certidumbre de su próximo fin le transformaba; sin duda, obraba en su espíritu como la enfermedad en su organismo, devorándolo, con efectos semejantes a los del fuego, y reduciéndolo a cenizas. Su voz quejumbrosa despertaba en cuantos le oían una emoción profunda. El genio quisquilloso y las expresiones groseras y disonantes ya no atormentaban a la familia y servidumbre.[38] Todo era concordia, lástima, perdón, cariño. Tal beneficio había hecho la muerte con sólo llamar a la puerta del pecador. Agobiado éste por el mal que de hora en hora le iba consumiendo, apenas tenía fuerzas para articular palabras breves, de ternura para su hija y para Cruz, de bondad paternal para las demás personas que le rodeaban. No se movía; su cara terrosa hundíase en las almohadas, y en la cara los ojos, con los cuales hablaba más que con la lengua. Creyérase que con ellos imploraba el perdón de su egoísmo. Y con ellos parecía decir también: "Os lo entrego todo, mi alma y mis riquezas, mi conciencia y mi carácter, para que hagáis de ello lo que queráis. Ya no soy nada, ya no valgo

nada. Heme vuelto polvo, y como polvo os pido que sopléis en mí para lanzarme al viento y difundirme por los espacios." (*OC*, 1184)

That Torquemada's docility and his seeming repentance are motivated by his fear is confirmed by the narrator when he comments that when Torquemada received Holy Communion: 'Expresaba un respeto hondo, una cortedad de genio que rayaba en pueril timidez, una compunción indefinible, que lo mismo podía significar todas las ternezas del alma que todos los terrores del instinto' (*OC*, 1185). The narrator notes that Gamborena does not miss the opportunity provided by Torquemada's malleability in order to ensure his control over him:

Aprovechó éste [Gamborena] la buena ocasión que la relativa tranquilidad del enfermo le ofrecía y exhortándole con su palabra persuasiva y cariñosa [. . .] a la media hora le había puesto tan blando que nadie le conocía [. . .] Descansó después algunas horas y a la madrugada volvió el padrito a cogerle por su cuenta, temeroso de que se le fuera de entre las manos. Pero no, bien asegurado estaba, humilde y con timidez mimosa de niño enfermo, descompuesto el carácter, del cual sólo quedaban escorias, destruida su salvaje independencia. (*OC*, 1184)

In order to gain control over Torquemada, Gamborena needs to secure his docility, which the narrator contrasts with the 'salvaje independencia' that characterizes him. The ex-missionary fears to lose Torquemada's soul ('temeroso de que se le fuera de entre las manos'). It is as important for Gamborena to secure Torquemada's conversion as it is for Torquemada to ensure his survival in the afterlife. Neither of them can afford to waste the opportunity of making a profit. Galdós was eager to stress, throughout this episode, the calculating manner in which both Torquemada and Gamborena are determined to fight their own personal battles to the very last minute. In the novel, and particularly after Torquemada falls seriously ill, Gamborena is shown to take every chance to win the sick Torquemada's will.[39] But Gamborena's 'saving' mission proves to be a difficult one, and he constantly has to face Torquemada's unruly and defiant behaviour and his unwillingness to accept God's will.

Thus, later on in the episode, when after a treacherous and deceptive recovery there is another relapse in his illness, Torquemada cannot resign himself to dying. In spite of the seriousness of his condition, he is hopeful that he will live and, what is more important to him, that he will be able to continue with his debt conversion project. When Gamborena urges him to ask for forgiveness for his sins it is evident that Torquemada's mind is far from thinking about contrition and death, to Gamborena's despair:

> De improviso abrió el infeliz Torquemada los ojos, y como si nada hubiera oído de lo que su confesor le decía, salió por otro registro [. . .]:
>
> —Estoy muy débil . . ., pero con los reparos saldré adelante, y no me muero, no me muero. Ya tengo bien calculadas las combinaciones de la conversión . . . (*OC*, 1192)

However, when he realizes that the chances of a recovery are slim, he becomes intractable and uncooperative, showing no clear signs of remorse. Torquemada's rebellious spirit and his failure to repent genuinely are Gamborena's major concerns; his lack of guilt undermines the priest's control over his penitent. It is this resistance to admit his sins that will prompt Gamborena to take drastic action. At this point in the narrative, Gamborena sees himself as someone who is in a battle and needs to regain the position he has lost to the enemy, whereas Torquemada is likened to the booty almost lost in that same battle. He is also equated with a prey on which the strong-willed Gamborena intends to feed: 'Testarudo era el misionero, y no se dejaría quitar tan fácilmente la presa', the narrator points out (*OC*, 1193). This is illustrative not only of Gamborena's 'hunting' instincts and his need to secure Torquemada's soul but also of his perception of Torquemada as a wild animal, the association of the lower classes with animality and savagery being of relevance here.[40]

The narrator continues to use military imagery throughout this episode. Gamborena, wary of the advantages won by his enemy, is now on full alert, and prepares a strategic plan to defeat his opponent. As the narrator remarks: 'El buen sacerdote se preparó a luchar como un león; examinado el terreno y elegidas las armas, se trazó un plan' (*OC*, 1193). Furthermore, Gamborena's military talents are paralleled to the qualities he displays as a businessman. The narrator observes that Gamborena was an expert in the business of saving souls ('hombre de mucha práctica en aquellos negocios' (*OC*, 1193)), emphasizing his business-oriented spirit. Indeed, in attempting to save Torquemada's soul, Gamborena conducts himself as if he were engaged in a military operation or in a business deal, drawing up a strategic plan of action and making sure that he moves the correct pieces in order to remain in the winning side at all costs, even if this means acting with cruelty and selfishness and telling Torquemada the whole truth about his condition. In Gamborena's view, Torquemada's obsession with accumulating riches is getting in the way of his conversion. Thus, the only way of winning him to his cause is to disclose to him that there is no hope: he should forget about his plans on earth and prepare himself to die in a Christian way. Torquemada's reaction to the discovery of his real situation is described forcefully and vividly:

> Fue como un hachazo. Creyó que debía darlo, y lo dio sin consideración alguna. Para Torquemada fue como si una mano de formidable fuerza le apretara el cuello. Puso los ojos en blanco, soltó de su boca un sordo mugido, y cuerpo y cabeza se hundieron más en las blanduras del lecho, o al menos pareció que se hundían. [. . .] Abatidos los párpados, fruncido el entrecejo, la boca fuertemente cerrada, chafando un labio contra otro, el enfermo se desfiguró visiblemente en breve tiempo. Su piel era como papel de estraza y despedía un olor ratonil, síntoma comúnmente observado en la muerte por hambre. (*OC,* 1193–4)

The powerful images used in this passage to describe Torquemada's distraught state and his terror before the proximity of death have the effect of arousing the reader's pity and commiseration for this character and, at the same time, of making him/her wary of Gamborena's intentions. Gamborena has no doubts in depriving Torquemada of hope as long as he does not lose his prey. In doing so, he is acting with the very selfishness and lack of consideration and humanity of which he accuses Torquemada, something which cannot go unnoticed by the reader.[41] Ironically, Gamborena's tactic seems to backfire on him, as it precipitates Torquemada's death. After this blow, Torquemada's spirits flag, he seems to have no will of his own and half-loses consciousness. His remorse becomes, if anything, more doubtful. In spite of the fact that Torquemada tells Gamborena that he admits and confesses his sins, he says it without enthusiasm, and his words are barely perceptible. For him it is a mere formality with which he needs to comply in order to safeguard his soul for eternity. Thus, straight after 'admitting' his sins, he tells Gamborena that he must open the gates of heaven for him, otherwise he will stay in this world in order to carry out his business: 'Pero ¿usted abre? . . . Dígame si abre. Porque si no . . ., aquí me quedo, y . . . A bien que no es floja empresa . . . convertir el Exterior y las Cubas en Interior . . .' (*OC*, 1194).

Gamborena, who is described as 'desconsolado y lleno de inquietud', prepares now to engage in a fierce battle with the devil, whom he imagines 'luchando encarnizadamente'. The narrative at this point abounds in war-like images and terms, such as 'formidable batalla', 'tremenda lucha', 'enemigo', 'vencer', 'salir victorioso', 'puesto de combate' and 'campo de batalla'. But Torquemada does not seem aware of what goes on around him, as he never fully recovers consciousness. The narrator notes that there is a point at which Torquemada is unable to recognize either Gamborena or the *hermanita de la caridad* who accompanies the priest at Torquemada's death-bed. Also, he does not seem to understand Gamborena's words. The priest's unease at the expression of suspicion and distrust in the eyes of the moribund Torquemada is highlighted by the narrator.[42] There is indeed a great amount of uncertainty surrounding Torquemada's final moments. The nun tries to bring Torquemada to accept the Catholic faith, but the text, by drawing attention to the ambiguity of Torquemada's words and actions, and his lack of awareness of what is happening around him, suggests that the attempts to regain control over Torquemada are in vain:

> la monjita le decía con ferviente anhelo que invocase a Jesús, y mostrándole un crucifijo de bronce lo aplicó a sus labios para que lo besara. No se pudo asegurar que lo hiciera, porque el movimiento de los labios fue imperceptible. Cuando le administraron la Extremaunción no se dio cuenta de ello el enfermo. Poco después tuvo otro momento de relativa lucidez, y a las exhortaciones de la monjita respondió quizá de un modo inconsciente:
>
> —Jesús, Jesús y yo . . ., buenos amigos . . . Quiero salvarme. (*OC*, 1195)

It should be taken into account that when Torquemada utters these words, his 'lucidez' is described as 'relativa' and that the narrator adds that he may have been half-conscious when he spoke. Still, Gamborena holds on desperately to this last chance of winning Torquemada's soul. The priest is, however, left in doubt regarding Torquemada's feelings and thoughts, as he is unable to interpret Torquemada's mutterings. The ambiguity remains:

> Algunas expresiones, mugidos o simples fenómenos acústicos del aliento resbalando entre los labios, o del aire en la laringe, los tradujo Gamborena con vario criterio. Unas veces, confiado y optimista, traducía: "Jesús . . ., salvación . . ., perdón . . ." Otras, pesimista y desperanzado, tradujo: "la llave . . ., venga la llave . . . Exterior . . ., mi capa . . ., tres por ciento." (*OC*, 1195–6)

A few minutes before his death there is one last moment of ambiguity, when Torquemada utters the word 'conversión'. Although the nun interprets this word as a clear sign of Torquemada's conversion to true Catholicism, the more realistic Gamborena does not share the naive nun's enthusiasm, being aware of the double meaning that the term has for Torquemada:

> A la madrugada, seguros ya los dos religiosos de que se acercaba el fin, redoblaron su celo de agonizantes, y cuando la monjita le exhortaba con gran vehemencia a repetir los nombres de Jesús y María y a besar el santo crucifijo, el pobre tacaño se despidió de este mundo diciendo con voz muy perceptible:
>
> —Conversión.
>
> Algunos minutos después de decirlo volvió aquella alma su rostro hacia la eternidad.
>
> —¡Ha dicho conversión!—observó la monjita con alegría [. . .]. Ha querido decir que se convierte, que . . .
>
> Palpando la frente del muerto, Gamborena daba fríamente esta respuesta:
>
> —¡Conversión! ¿Es la de su alma o la de la Deuda?
>
> La monjita no comprendió bien el concepto, y ambos, de rodillas, se pusieron a rezar. (*OC*, 1196)

This scene is highly reminiscent of the ambiguity with which Galdós presents Mauricia *la dura*'s death. The ambiguities and contradictions that surround Mauricia's repentance persist to the very moment of her death, where there is a humorous passage in which those who are present at her death-bed doubt whether the alcoholic Mauricia died saying that she could already see the other world, as some of those at her death-bed seem to think, or

asking for more sherry, as doña Lupe, more realistically, assures.
As the latter relates to Fortunata:

> Luego la vimos mover los labios y sacar la punta de la lengua como
> si quisiera relamerse . . . Dejo oír una voz que parecía venir, por un
> tubo, del sótano de la casa. A mí me pareció que dijo: *más, más* . . .
> Otras personas que allí había aseguran que dijo: *ya.* Como quien
> dice: 'Ya veo la gloria y los ángeles'. Bobería; no dijo sino *más* . . . a
> saber, *más Jerez.* (II, 224–5)

Although Torquemada's repentance in this last novel of the
series is presented on the surface in an ambiguous way, for any
reader who has followed his trajectory from his first appearance
in *Torquemada en la hoguera* to the moment of his death, it would
be difficult, if not naive, to conclude that Torquemada does, at
the last moment, repent his sins. Surely it could only have been
the conversion of the debt that the moribund Torquemada had in
his mind immediately before parting with the world. Yet, the issue
of Torquemada's condemnation or salvation is not one that
concerned Galdós. The focus of attention in this last novel of the
series is, rather, the *negocio de intercambio* between the missionary
and the penitent, an exchange deal in which both parties, as
Galdós has clearly demonstrated, intend to make a profit. And in
this *operación mercantil* Gamborena is unmistakably on the losing
side. The ex-missionary's attempts at coercion fail, and he does
not achieve his aim of converting Torquemada. The fact that
Torquemada is not responsive to Gamborena constitutes not
merely an authorial comment on the miser's lack of spiritual
feelings and on his business- and profit-oriented mentality – as
critics have often argued – but also a criticism of Gamborena's
self-interested attempts to exercise control over Torquemada. It
cannot be denied that Torquemada is calculating and materialistic, but it is also true that in the episode of his illness and death he
often appears as a victim of the authoritarian and manipulative
Gamborena. Also, Torquemada's lack of understanding of his
salvation as nothing but a business deal, that is, his rational
approach to death, is often presented in a humorous way, which
has the effect of eliciting a sympathetic response from the reader.
Gamborena's attitude to the whole affair is, by contrast, presented
much more mercilessly.

NOTES

1   Geraldine Scanlon, 'Torquemada: "Becerro de oro"', *Modern Language Notes*, 91, 1 (1976), 264–76.

2   Even his wife Fidela is shown to perceive him as a beast, in spite of her affectionate tone.

3   According to Social Darwinist discourse, economic competition made winners of those who could survive the rigours of the free market, a process that deposited a 'residue' of the 'unfit' at the bottom of society. Members of this 'residuum' were seen as inherently unable to help themselves, not just because they were prevented from doing so by their adverse environment but because of biological and psychological degeneracy. As such, they became increasingly identified with 'primitive tribes' and 'savages', their culture of poverty and immorality inbred and perpetuated. See, in this respect, Jose Harris, 'Between civic virtue and Social Darwinism: The concept of the residuum', in David Englander and Rosemary O'Day (eds), *Retrieved Riches: Social Investigation in Britain* (Aldershot: Scolar Press, 1995), pp. 67–87, 67. Within this context, it is ironic that Torquemada, who is shown to be perfectly adapted to survival in the modern, competitive city, should be perceived as a 'savage' by Gamborena and other characters in the series. Galdós reinforces the irony by highlighting Torquemada's view of himself as a city-dwelling type, who, as we saw in Chapter 1, feels out of place in the countryside, 'unfit' to survive in rural life, where economic competition and the pace of life were less stark.

4   Daniel Pick, *Faces of Degeneration* (Cambridge: Cambridge University Press, 1993), p. 39.

5   Ibid., pp. 37–44.

6   Jacques Donzelot, *The Policing of Families: Welfare Versus the State* (London: Hutchinson and Co. Ltd., 1980), p. 55.

7   Pick, p. 37.

8   Benito Pérez Galdós, *Fortunata y Jacinta*, 2 vols, ed. by Francisco Caudet (Madrid: Cátedra, 1983), vol. 1, 265. Further references are to this edition, and are given in the main body of the text.

9   I have explored the controlling aim of Guillermina's philanthropic activities in *Visions of Filth: Deviancy and Social Control in the Novels of Galdós* (Liverpool: Liverpool University Press, 2003), particularly chs 1 and 2.

10 H. Peseux-Richard, a contemporary of Galdós, commented on Gamborena's self-satisfaction and vanity, totally unsuited to a missionary. See his review of *Torquemada y San Pedro*, *Revue Hispanique*, 2 (1895), 197–8.

11 Scanlon ('Torquemada: "Becerro de oro"', 275) has commented on how the presentation of Gamborena as an actor conscious of the need to impress his audience in this scene represents an ironic authorial comment on the priest's vanity.

12 It needs to be remembered that Guillermina was also portrayed as an

efficient and calculating 'business woman'. The episode of the purchase of Pitusín, out of which Guillermina makes a substantial profit, offers a good example of this. As Denah Lida has pointed out in this respect ('Galdós y sus santas modernas', *Anales Galdosianos*, X [1975], 19–31, 25), Guillermina is often involved in *negocios de intercambio*.

13 Scanlon, 'Torquemada: "Becerro de oro"', 275; and Joaquín Casalduero, *Vida y obra de Galdós*, 3rd edn (Madrid: Gredos, 1970), p. 119.

14 Benito Pérez Galdós, *Obras Completas* (Madrid, 1912), vol. 1, p. 274, as quoted by Scanlon, 'Torquemada: "Becerro de oro"', 265.

15 The character of Torquemada, born into the lower ranks of society, does not fit neatly into the stereotyped image that the middle classes had of the 'immoral' lower classes, as he has some precepts, such as sobriety, temperance and hard work, which have traditionally been associated with the bourgeoisie. Although Torquemada is shown to take hard work and thrift to ridiculous extremes, it should be conceded that he is presented as a sober and temperate man (the assertion made by the narrator that: 'El, ni bebida; él, ni mujeres; él, ni juego; él, ni tan siquiera el inofensivo placer del tabaco' (*OC*, 971) is relevant in this respect), which redeems the savage and animalistic traits that members of the upper classes ascribe to the miser. It could also be argued that Torquemada's ingenuity and business talents detract from the assumption, in anthropological discourses, of the intellectual inferiority of both the lower layers of the population and 'uncivilized' peoples in primitive societies. Gamborena's pigeonholing of Torquemada as 'uncivilized' and 'immoral' exposes the philanthropist's use and adaptation of contemporary anthropological discourse on the survival of an uncivilized element within urban society to his own 'reformatory' purposes.

16 In this episode, by using the comparison between 'moral' status and socio-economic status, Gamborena could also be seen as playing cynically on Torquemada's insecurity regarding his social status. This reinforces, once more, the priest's ruthless and inhuman attitude.

17 An example of this is also seen in the relationship between the philanthropist Guillermina and working-class characters, notably, Fortunata, Mauricia and Izquierdo, in *Fortunata y Jacinta*, where the narrator leaves no doubts regarding Guillermina's position in the moral hierarchy.

18 Donzelot, p. 57.

19 Ibid., p. 65.

20 The writer and philanthropist Concepción Arenal was fully aware of the philanthropist's need to legitimize her activities, as feelings of resentment and hostility could arise from her interference. She thus advised tact and diplomacy when dealing with the poor. See her *El visitador del pobre*, 1860, in *Obras Completas*, 2 vols, ed. by Carmen Díaz Castañón (Madrid: Atlas [Biblioteca de Autores Españoles], 1993), vol. 1, p. 17.

21 See, for instance, Anne Summers, 'A home from home – women's

philanthropic work in the nineteenth century', in Sandra Burman (ed.), *Fit Work for Women* (London: Croom Helm, 1979), pp. 33–63, 45–6.

[22] Torquemada's impatience and unwillingness to speak to Gamborena in this scene are reminiscent of the interview between Guillermina and the working-class Izquierdo, who is similarly shown to be reluctant to receive the philanthropist's visit and accepts her interference unwillingly. As the narrator remarks, Izquierdo 'ya estaba seguro de que Guillermina le volvería tarumba con sus *tiologías*' (I, 368). (Interestingly, in the same way as Torquemada uses the derogatory 'tío' to refer to Gamborena, the malapropism 'tiologías' used by Izquierdo seems to be a humorous mixture of 'teologías' and 'tía'.) The mistrust that Gamborena is said to arouse in Torquemada is not different either from the suspicion with which Izquierdo regarded Guillermina. Also, both in *Torquemada y San Pedro* and *Fortunata y Jacinta* the philanthropist's verbal superiority alienates the recipient by reinforcing the inferior position that he occupies in the moral hierarchy. Thus, in *Fortunata y Jacinta*, the narrator points out that: 'Desde que se cruzaron las primeras palabras de aquella conferencia [. . .] cayó Izquierdo en la cuenta de que tenía que habérselas con un diplomático mucho más fuerte que él' (I, 368), whereas Torquemada is said to feel 'abrumado por la elocuencia contundente del bendito clérigo' (*OC*, 1155). Both Gamborena and Guillermina use their verbal ability as an instrument of control.

[23] In *Fortunata y Jacinta*, Izquierdo is also seen trying to make a profit out of Guillermina's interference.

[24] Constancio Bernaldo de Quirós and José M. Llanas Aguilaneido, *La mala vida en Madrid* (Madrid: B. Rodríguez Serra, 1901), p. 345.

[25] Don Carlos, in the novel *Misericordia*, is an obvious example of this traditional conception of charity, which still survived in late nineteenth-century Spain. As we shall see, in the *Torquemada* series Galdós's criticism of those who try to buy their entry to heaven is not only directed towards Torquemada but also towards Gamborena, who tries to save his soul through the conversion of Torquemada. Although Gamborena is not portrayed in the same negative light as don Carlos, Galdós provides plenty of evidence of the priest's calculating and selfish ways.

[26] See, for instance, Concepción Arenal, *El pauperismo*, 2 vols (Madrid: Librería de Victoriano Suárez, 1897), vol. 1, p. 381 ff.; and *La Voz de la Caridad* (15 May 1880). Public health experts also commented often on the issue of poverty and mendicity, which they regarded, in the same way as alcoholism, prostitution, insanity and criminality, as a social disease that represented a threat to the moral health of the nation.

[27] Torquemada, as we saw, prides himself on having risen from poverty thanks to his virtues, such as self-improvement, hard work, thrift and temperance – which significantly coincide with those values traditionally seen as a preserve of the bourgeoisie. Of course, some of these values are shown to be taken to such extremes that they turn into

vices. As we saw in Chapter 1, through Torquemada's exaggerated display of hard work and thrift Galdós pokes fun at the idea of the self-made man and the promotion of 'respectable' values by the bourgeoisie.

28 Deep down Torquemada believes that his intention to assist the poor has inclined God's will in his favour, and that this is the reason for his recovery. On suffering a relapse, he feels that God has not fulfilled his part of the deal, hence his vindictive reaction to Gamborena.

29 Another example of Gamborena's use of business terms is his reference, in this passage, to the 'negocio del alma'.

30 John H. Sinnigen ('Literary and ideological projects in Galdós: The *Torquemada* series', *Ideologies and Literature*, 3, 11 [1979], 5–19, 7, 11) has written that although Gamborena is seen to endorse traditional religious beliefs against Torquemada's, condemning the usurer's avarice, he is portrayed, in effect, as representative of 'the church at the service of capital'.

31 It is noteworthy that in *Self-Help* Smiles devotes a section to missionaries, whose energy, courage and tenacity he praises. It is also significant, in respect of the link between the military man and the missionary drawn by Galdós, that Smiles should draw a parallel between 'heroes of the sword' and 'heroes of the gospel': see Samuel Smiles, *Self-Help* (1859) (London: John Murray, 1958), pp. 241–3. In his book, Smiles provides a long list of self-made men who are essentially portrayed as heroes, having achieved great things for the nation. Similarly, Galdós's ex-missionary is seen congratulating himself for having won for God 'portions of land and humanity as large as Spain' (*OC*, 1119). It is obvious that Gamborena regards himself as a hero and on occasions is portrayed as such by the narrator, although, as we have seen, this description is often undermined by the use of irony.

32 Frank Prochaska, *The Voluntary Impulse: Philanthropy in Modern Britain* (London: Faber & Faber, 1988), p. 24.

33 The disruptive and unruly Mauricia is expelled from the convent of Las Micaelas when the nuns and Guillermina fail to discipline her. Later on, after she is badly injured and is nearing death, Guillermina makes one final attempt to 'reform' her by making her recant.

34 Prochaska observes in this regard, that Christianity originated with a death, and was sustained by death. Common in nineteenth-century life and literature is the death-bed scene, with the dying surrounded by women visitors, emblematic of the motherly and female anguish at the foot of the cross. See Frank Prochaska, *Women and Philanthropy in Nineteenth-Century England* (Oxford: Clarendon Press, 1980), p. 160.

35 Generating guilt is part of what Michel Foucault qualified as 'subtle' or more sophisticated instruments of control, by virtue of the fact that the individual's mind is placed under continual coercion. Foucault related how self-control in the lunatic asylum was assisted by the self-acknowledgement of guilt on the part of the inmate. The inmate was made to feel 'morally responsible for everything (within him) which may disturb morality and society, and must hold no one

but himself responsible or the punishment he receives' (*Madness and Civilization: A History of Insanity in the Age of Reason* [London: Routledge, 1992], pp. 246–7). Therefore, fear of punishment was seen as an efficient and not overbearing means of controlling patients.

[36] Prochaska (*Women and Philanthropy*, pp. 155–7), who concentrates on the relationship between the female philanthropist and the prostitute (a main target of women's philanthropy in the late nineteenth century), has observed that the prostitute's unwillingness to confess her sins was particularly disturbing to women visitors.

[37] Earlier in the novel the narrator notes that his tenderness was a symptom of his illness (of the hypochondria of which he was a victim), and he refers to its exaggerated manifestations as 'verdaderos ataques' (*OC*, 1163).

[38] Torquemada's use of vulgar language is reminiscent of Mauricia's filthy vocabulary in *Fortunata y Jacinta*, and particularly in the episode when she is nearing her death. Both in Torquemada's and Mauricia's case, the use of foul language is indicative of the sinners' non-compliance with the philanthropist's wishes and their refusal to yield to their control.

[39] That Gamborena does not waste any opportunity to win Torquemada's will is illustrated earlier in the episode, in a passage in which the narrator relates how the sick Torquemada enjoyed listening to Gamborena's stories about his time as a missionary in distant countries, and how the priest took advantage of this: 'Y creyendo Gamborena que, aprisionada la imaginación del enfermo, fácil le sería cautivar su voluntad, referíale estupendos episodios de su poema evangélico' (*OC*, 1176).

[40] In this respect, it is noteworthy that on various occasions in *Fortunata y Jacinta* Guillermina is also portrayed as a 'hunter'. When Mauricia has a mental fit and has to leave the house of the Protestant pastor and his wife, the narrator remarks that Guillermina 'le echa un cordel al pescuezo y se la lleva' (II, 167). Also, the narrator tells us that Guillermina had 'hunted' in the streets a good number of the *recogidas* of the convent of las Micaelas (I, 628).

[41] For instance, when Torquemada asks for guarantees of the existence of the afterlife, Gamborena replies, in a recriminatory way: 'usted, como buen egoísta, quiere que vaya por delante la seguridad de ganancia' (*OC*, 1157).

[42] The unease shown by Gamborena in this episode, and his insistent attempts to make Torquemada repent his sins, recall Guillermina's efforts against all odds to persuade Fortunata to reject her 'idea' on her death-bed. Both examples serve to illustrate the philanthropist's fear and anxiety over losing control of the penitent's will.

Conclusion

Galdós was writing in an age when ideas on profit and waste were rampant, when a spirit of utility was rife. The notion of 'waste versus profit' and a belief in scientific rationalism pervaded contemporary discourses on racial degeneration and the *value* of life, on political economy and the connected idea of utility, on self-help, on philanthropy, and on poverty and charity. All of these debates had a profound impact on the novels of the *Torquemada* series, in which ideas of 'waste versus profit', both at *national* and *individual* levels, abound.

At a *national*, or *social*, level the *Torquemada* novels bear witness to contemporary anxieties regarding the squandering of human resources, or intellectual and human capital, through the effects of racial degeneration, disease and death. The series is peppered with examples of characters who exhibit symptoms of what Galdós's contemporaries would have regarded as 'degenerative' diseases. The issue of degeneration is not addressed, however, in either a consistent or systematic way. Although the novels of the series echo some common beliefs on racial degeneration, at the same time they question the validity of the degeneration doctrine by subverting some of its basic principles and premises, notably the link between degeneration and a diseased heredity. Through the use of irony, Galdós often satirizes exaggerated fears and concerns about the degeneration of the race, and the damaging effects that this could have on population growth, productivity and national wealth. The main irony in this respect is the death through meningitis of the genius Valentín (whose potential productivity and 'usefulness' to the nation is emphasized by Torquemada) and his 'replacement' by Valentín II, who is not only a degenerate, and therefore economically unproductive, but is also presented as wasteful. The birth of the cretin Valentín is particularly ironic if one takes into account that Donoso, the champion

of industrial advancement and social progress, had urged Torquemada to remarry in order to produce 'useful citizens' for society.
Furthermore, from the perspective of the contemporary perception of suicide as a 'theft' inflicted on the nation's wealth by
individuals who take their own life, Rafael's suicide at the end of
Torquemada en el purgatorio also strikes one as deeply ironic,
because the blind Rafael's life was far from being productive.

The spirit of 'waste versus profit' at an *individual* level has a
clear manifestation in the exchange mentality which dominates
the series, and of which Torquemada is one (but by no means the
only) example. In addition to reflecting Galdós's critical engagement with contemporary discourses on racial degeneration, the
death of Torquemada's first son and the birth of the second
Valentín are an obvious example of Galdós's mocking criticism of
Torquemada's spirit of utility and profit; that is, of his incapacity
to comprehend the notion of *giving* (the life of the first Valentín)
without *receiving* something in return (the birth of another genius
as a compensation for the loss of the first). In Torquemada's
utilitarian mind, nothing must be wasted: in the same way that
leftovers and cast-offs can be recycled, so can his son's life.

Torquemada firmly believes that the relationship between
humans and God, like the relationship between humans themselves, is ruled by a *give-and-take* culture. For Torquemada there is
no *giving* without *taking* in all paths of life. His reaction to the
proximity of his death is not dissimilar to the calculating tactics he
deploys when the genius Valentín falls seriously ill. After
Valentín's death there is, however, a difference of approach, as
Torquemada learns the lesson that he must be suspicious of
making deals that do not yield benefits. Thus, when Fidela's life is
threatened, Torquemada refuses to pray, because he can have no
certainty that the prayers will spare her life ('para que no me
dejen con un palmo de narices, como en el caso de Valentín . . .'
(*OC,* 1144), Torquemada thinks to himself). Later, when his own
life is threatened, he adopts the same attitude, badgering Gamborena to secure the salvation of his soul before committing
himself to surrendering his fortune to the poor, a deal which may
be wasteful to him.

The theme of charity and poverty, which is the common
denominator in the first and last novels of the series, constitutes a
clear manifestation of Torquemada's give-and-take mentality. In
both novels Torquemada *needs* the poor, or to *give* to the poor, in

order to *obtain* a tangible benefit (Valentín's life in the first novel of the series and his own survival in the afterlife in the last). He is only inclined to charity when it presents itself as an opportunity to gain something. An obvious example of this in the first novel of the series is the sequence in which the miser gives a beggar his old cape instead of his new one. When he returns home he exclaims: '¡Maldito de mí! No debí dejar escapar aquel acto de cristiandad' (*OC*, 921). Torquemada clearly associates charity-giving with an opportunity to make a profit by using 'dejar escapar' – normally followed by the object 'oportunidad' – with 'acto de cristiandad'. In both the first and the fourth novels of the series, Torquemada is shown to regard the poor as fundamentally wasteful. His rational attitude to charity and poverty is in keeping with those of contemporary moral and social commentators, philanthropists and government officials who, influenced by the pragmatic and utilitarian spirit of the age, regarded the (undeserving) poor as improvident, dissolute and a drain on national resources. By raising the issue of charity, Galdós was not simply exposing Torquemada's moral shortcomings, but was also bringing to the fore a burning debate of the time: the issue of wasteful, indiscriminate charity versus rational-scientific charity.

But the protagonist is not the only victim of the give-and-take mentality that permeates the series. If Torquemada attempts to make a deal with Gamborena in order to save his soul for eternity, the priest turns the sinner's conversion into a business intended for his own 'spiritual' profit. Galdós exposes philanthropy as an exercise of control, driven by rational and pragmatic pursuits. Gamborena, an enterprising, 'self-made' man of the Church, is guided, as much as Torquemada, by the give-and-take mentality and is determined not to waste any opportunity to save Torquemada's soul after having made a 'spiritual' investment in him. Through the use of irony, humour and narrative technique the text undermines the approving presentation of the priest. Gamborena is indeed portrayed as being prey to the same defects he accuses Torquemada of possessing: not only is he calculating, self-seeking and business-oriented, he is also shown to be insensitive, cruel and inhuman – specifically in the passage where, aware that he may lose control over Torquemada, he decides to tell him the truth about his imminent death. In the episode dealing with his illness and death, Torquemada is described as a victim of the coercive tactics of the manipulative Gamborena, who tries to instil fear in him as a main instrument of control. Ironically, Gamborena's influence on Torquemada is minimal if we compare it, for instance, to the hold that Bailón, Donoso or Cruz have over him in the series, which does not say much for the priest and his philanthropic endeavours.

In the *Torquemada* series everything becomes a transaction. There is not much difference between the exchange deal that takes place between Gamborena and Torquemada in *Torquemada y San Pedro*, and the contract in *Torquemada en la cruz* between Torquemada and the Aguila sisters, in which Torquemada similarly appears to be manipulated by others. Galdós is eager to stress the contractual nature of this marriage arrangement by drawing attention to the fact that Torquemada is unaware to the last moment of which of the two sisters he is marrying, as Donoso, the marriage 'broker', does not reach that 'stage of the negotiations', as he puts it, until the end. Torquemada is shown to be fully aware of the absurd 'blind marriage' Donoso has driven him into, with hardly any involvement in his part, and reacts against his mentor's cold and business-like approach to his future union.

As a result of the marriage deal, Torquemada is again on the losing side, completely intimidated and dominated by his imperious sister-in-law. It is no coincidence that Donoso talks about Torquemada's marriage to the Aguila sisters, as if he were to marry both, as Torquemada humorously remarks. In fact, it is Cruz who acts as the real wife, taking all the relevant decisions regarding domestic and financial matters. Fidela and Torquemada are fully dependent on Cruz, feeling obliged to submit to her overbearing control. The psychological torture that Cruz inflicts upon Torquemada is emphasized in the text of *Torquemada en el purgatorio*. Indeed, the miserable life that Torquemada is forced to live is presented as one of the determining factors of his rapidly deteriorating health. Torquemada's submissiveness and docility, along with his futile resistance to Cruz's mandates (he is aware that he is fighting a losing battle against his sister-in-law) have the effect of arousing the reader's pity for him. Torquemada's perception of himself as an exemplary self-made man, and in particular his obsession with economizing, may be mocked by Galdós, but the author's criticism of Cruz's unbridled squandering and constant draining of Torquemada's finances is even more merciless. In the same way that in the last novel of the series

Torquemada is prey to the authoritative, domineering and self-interested Gamborena, in *Torquemada en el purgatorio* he is described as a victim of the self-seeking and dictatorial Cruz. Like Gamborena, Cruz enters into a contractual agreement with Torquemada from which she expects to extract benefit. The audacity with which she manages and draws on a fortune which she unscrupulously appropriates, testifies to her shrewd and manipulative nature.[1] Cruz and Gamborena, the two characters engaged in Torquemada's 'conversion' in *Torquemada y San Pedro*, are shown to be as aggressively profit-seeking as the protagonist.[2]

The double-edged presentation of Torquemada is also seen in the author's subversion of the perception that the upper classes, and the narrator himself, have of Torquemada as an animal and a 'savage'. Torquemada, although from humble origins, does not fit neatly into the middle-class perception of the lower classes as lacking in moral traits. On the contrary, he displays respectable values, such as sobriety, temperance, independence, self-improvement, hard work and thrift, which were traditionally held to be bourgeois in complexion.[3] Of course, Torquemada does not always channel these values in the right direction, and in fact takes some of them to such an extreme that they assume the status of a vice. Although Torquemada's zeal for hard work and thrift are satirized by Galdós, it should be conceded that he is described as a sober, provident and temperate man. Contemporary social and moral commentators often stressed weak character and the 'innate' moral failings of the lower classes as the main determinant of their destitution (an attitude which insists on the need to indoctrinate the poor). If we take into consideration that the aim of philanthropy was to reform the character and immoral habits of their social inferiors through the imposition of bourgeois moral values, it is ironic that Torquemada should be shown to display some of these respectable qualities. From this perspective, the contemporary belief that irreligiousness was the main cause of socially reprehensible behaviour – notably drinking, improvidence, idleness and neglect of work – and as such at the root of destitution, is discredited.[4]

Torquemada's perceived moral inferiority, likewise his ignorance and gullibility, make him the target of attempts to mould and control him, which explains the succession of 'mentors' at different stages of the series. For all his defects, Torquemada is often portrayed as a docile and defenceless puppet in the hands of stronger, domineering characters.[5] Bailón, Donoso, Cruz and Gamborena all try to influence and control him. In the *Torquemada* novels, the protagonist often appears as a naive and passive recipient of the ideas of others. The unfavourable presentation of the various controlling characters undercuts the negative judgement of Torquemada in the texts by drawing the reader's sympathy towards the miser.[6] Furthermore, the author's disapproval of his protagonist's rational and pragmatic spirit is tempered by the humorous presentation of his utilitarian and self-seeking pursuits and his over-rational approach to life and death.[7] This is not the case with other characters, notably Donoso, Gamborena and Cruz, who are the main target of the author's criticism. Galdós's dissatisfaction with the raw materialism of the utilitarian mentality should not be taken to mean that he dismissed materialism *per se*, seeking instead a residual spiritualism. On the contrary, he was a firm believer in the 'modern' and in the scientific, social and economic progress that this entailed.

NOTES

[1]   H. B. Hall ('Torquemada: The man and his language', in J. E. Varey [ed.], *Galdós Studies* [London: Tamesis, 1970], p. 154) has pointed out how Cruz uses Torquemada first as an instrument for the family's salvation from poverty and then as an instrument of her revenge.

[2]   Geraldine Scanlon ('Torquemada: "Becerro de oro"', *Modern Language Notes*, 91, 1 [1976], 264–76, 267) has observed that Cruz has, like Torquemada, an exaggerated sense of worth. As we saw in Chapter 3, this is also the case with Gamborena.

[3]   Countering the Marxist dominant ideology thesis, which assumes that the ideas and values of a dominant class are disseminated 'downwards' to other social groups in an attempt to maintain social order, it has been argued that values traditionally regarded as the preserve of the bourgeoisie (such as independence, individual effort, hard work, thrift and temperance) were not exclusively middle class but had a long tradition within the working classes. For a succinct critique of the dominant ideology thesis, see Nicholas Abercrombie, Stephen Hill and Bryan Turner, *The Dominant Ideology Thesis* (London: George Allen and Unwin), 1980.

[4]   The idea that the lack of religious feelings was responsible for the economic situation of the poor was expressed, among others, by the philanthropist Concepción Arenal.

[5]   In this respect Peter Earle ('Torquemada: hombre-masa', *Anales Galdosianos*, II [1967], 29–43, 36) has noted that from the moment of

doña Lupe's death Torquemada 'se deja llevar', abandoning his own will in order to carry out other people's wills: namely, those of doña Lupe (who advised him to marry into the Aguila family), Donoso and Cruz.

6 Also, Galdós harshly criticizes others who, like Donoso, represent the Madrid business and professional elite, an obvious example being the audience for Torquemada's speech in *Torquemada en el purgatorio*, who wildly applaud the speaker's ideas on self-help and progress.

7 Similarly, Torquemada's inability to acknowledge his defects, notably when asserting that he is an 'honest' man in his speech in *Torquemada en el purgatorio*, and when admitting to Gamborena that he has only virtues and is without sin, detract from the completely negative light in which the protagonist is viewed.

Bibliography

Works by Galdós

Angel Guerra, 2 vols (Madrid: Alianza, 1986).
Fortunata y Jacinta, 2 vols, ed. by Francisco Caudet (Madrid: Cátedra, 1983).
Halma, in Obras completas, vol. 5.
Nazarín (Madrid: Alianza, 1984).
Obras completas, 4th edn, vol. 5, ed. by Federico Carlos Sainz de Robles (Madrid: Aguilar, 1965).
Torquemada en la hoguera, in Obras completas, vol 5.
Torquemada en la cruz, in Obras completas, vol 5.
Torquemada en el purgatorio, in Obras completas, vol 5.
Torquemada y San Pedro, in Obras completas, vol 5.
Ghiraldo, Alberto (ed.), Obras inéditas de Benito Pérez Galdós, 10 vols (Madrid: Renacimiento, 1923–30).
Shoemaker, W. H. (ed.), Los artículos de Galdós en 'La Nación' (Madrid: Insula, 1972).
Shoemaker W. H. (ed.), Las cartas desconocidas de Galdós en 'La Prensa' de Buenos Aires (Madrid: Cultura Hispánica, 1973).

Other Works

Actas y Memorias del IX Congreso Internacional de Higiene y Demografía. Madrid, 10–17 abril de 1898. Enrique Salcedo Ginestral (ed.). 14 vols (Madrid: Imprenta de Ricardo Rojas, 1900).
Aldaraca, Bridget, El ángel del hogar: Galdós y la ideología de la domesticidad en España (Madrid: Visor, 1992).
Alvarez Peláez, Raquel, Sir Francis Galton, padre de la eugenesia (Madrid: C.S.I.C, 1985).
Arenal, Concepción, El pauperismo, 2 vols (Madrid: Librería de Victoriano Suárez, 1897).
—— El visitador del pobre (1860), in Obras Completas, 2 vols, ed. by Carmen Díaz Castañón (Madrid: Atlas [Biblioteca de Autores Españoles], 1993), vol. 1.
Baglietto, Mariano, 'Algunos datos estadísticos acerca del bocio y el cretinismo en la provincia de Asturias', in Actas del IX Congreso Internacional de Higiene y Demografía, vol. 12, pp. 241–3.

Ballester, Rosa and Emilio Balaguer, 'La infancia como valor y como problema en las luchas sanitarias de principios de siglo en España', *Dynamis*, 15 (1995), 177–92.

Bäuml, B. J. Zeidner, 'The mundane demon: The bourgeois grotesque in Galdós's *Torquemada en la hoguera*', *Symposium* XXIV (Summer 1970), 158–65.

Bell, Tom, 'Evolutionary theory in the *novelas contemporáneas* of Benito Pérez Galdós' (unpublished Ph.D. thesis, University of Sheffield, 2003).

Bentham, Jeremy, *The Panopticon; or, the Inspection-House* (1791), in John Bowring (ed.), *The Collected Works of Jeremy Bentham* (Edinburgh, 1843), IV, 39–172.

Bernaldo de Quirós, Constancio, and José M. Llanas Aguilaneido, *La mala vida en Madrid* (Madrid: B. Rodríguez Serra, 1901).

Bernheimer, Charles, *Figures of Ill Repute: Representing Prostitution in Nineteenth-Century France* (Cambridge, Mass.: Harvard University Press, 1989).

Boudreau, H. L., 'The salvation of Torquemada: Determinism and indeterminacy in the later novels of Galdós', *Anales Galdosianos*, XV (1980), 113–28.

Brierre de Boismont, A., *Du suicide et de la folie suicide* (Paris: Librairie Germer Baillière, 1865).

Briggs, Asa, '*Self-Help*: A Centenary Introduction', in Samuel Smiles, *Self-Help* (London: John Murray, 1958).

—— *Victorian People: A Reassessment of Persons and Themes 1851–67* (Harmondsworth: Penguin, 1965).

Burton, Wyndham H., *James Mill on philosophy and education* (London: Athlone Press, 1973).

Campos Marín, Ricardo, 'La teoría de la degeneración y la medicina social en España en el cambio de siglo', *Llull*, 21, 41 (1998), 333–56.

—— José Martínez Pérez and Rafael Huertas García-Alejo, *Los ilegales de la naturaleza. Medicina y degeneracionismo en la España de la Restauración (1876–1923)* (Madrid: C.S.I.C., 2001).

Casalduero, Joaquín, *Vida y obra de Galdós*, 2nd edn (Madrid: Gredos, 1961); and 3rd edn (Madrid: Gredos, 1970).

Cervera y Barat, Rafael, *Alcoholismo y civilización* (1898), in Antonio M. Rey González (ed.), pp. 107–28.

Cinquième Congrès international d'hygiène et de démographie à La Haye (du 21 au 27 août 1884). Comptes rendus et mémoires publiés par le Secrétaire Général. 2 tomes, La Haye, 1884.

Corbin, Alain, *Alexandre Parent-Duchâtelet: La Prostitution à Paris au XIX Siècle* (Paris: Seuil, 1981).

—— 'Commercial sexuality in nineteenth century France: A system of images and regulations', in Catherine Gallagher and Thomas Laqueur (eds), *The Making of the Modern Body: Sexuality and Society in the Nineteenth Century* (Berkeley and Los Angeles: University of California Press, 1987), pp. 209–19.

—— *The Foul and the Fragrant: Odor and the French Social Imagination* (Leamington Spa: Berg Publishers, 1986).

Correa, Gustavo, *El simbolismo religioso en las novelas de Pérez Galdós* (Madrid: Gredos, 1962).

Dendle, Brian, J., 'Albareda, Galdós and the *Revista de España* (1868–73)', in Clara E. Lida and Iris M. Zavala (eds), *La revolución de 1868: Historia, pensamiento, literatura* (New York: Las Américas, 1970), pp. 362–77.

Dickens, Charles, 'Idiots', *Household Words*, VII (4 June 1853), 313–17.

'Dirty Cleanliness', *Household Words*, XVIII (24 July 1858), 121–3.

Doncel, J., 'Causas que contribuyen a la mortalidad de los niños. Medios de remediarlas. Estadísticas comparativas', in *Actas del IX Congreso Internacional de Higiene y Demografía*, vol. 6, pp. 82–7.

Donzelot, Jacques, *The Policing of Families: Welfare Versus the State* (London: Hutchinson and Co. Ltd., 1980).

Earle, Peter G., 'Torquemada: hombre-masa', *Anales Galdosianos*, II (1967), 29–43.

Esquerdo, José María, *Locos que no lo parecen. Conferencia dada por el Dr Esquerdo en la Facultad de Medicina* (Madrid: Oficina Tipográfica del Hospicio, 1880).

——— 'Locos que no lo parecen. Garayo "El Sacamantecas"' (1881), in Antonio M. Rey González (ed.), pp. 199–237.

Esquirol, J. E. D., *Tratado completo de las enagenaciones mentales*, 2 vols (Madrid: Imprenta del Colegio de Surdo-Mudos, 1847). Tr. by Raimundo de Monasterio y Correa.

Fernández Caro, Angel, '¿Cuál es el concepto científico de las causas del cretinismo y qué medios pueden proponerse para combatir ese mal?', in *Estudios Críticos sobre el 6 Congreso Internacional de Higiene y Demografía de Viena* (Madrid: Imprenta de Infantería de Marina, 1888), pp. 385–90.

——— *Los deberes de la sociedad ante los intereses de la Higiene. Discursos leídos en la sesión inaugural del año académico de 1886–1887 en la Sociedad Española de Higiene, celebrada el día 27 de noviembre de 1886* (Madrid: Imprenta de Enrique Teodoro, 1886), pp. 3–43.

——— 'Discurso del académico [. . .] Angel Fernández-Caro y Nouvilas en contestación al discurso presentado por M. Tolosa, "Concepto y fines de la higiene popular"', in *Discursos leídos en la Real Academia de Medicina para la recepción pública del académico electo Manuel de Tolosa Latour* (Madrid: Est. Tip. de la Viuda e Hijos de Tello, 1900), pp. 47–68.

Fernández Juncos, Manuel (ed.), *Conferencias dominicales dadas en la Biblioteca Insular de Puerto Rico* (Temas: escuelas públicas, higiene, delincuencia, etc.) (San Juan de Puerto Rico: Bureau of Supplies, Ports, and Transportation, 1913).

Fernández y Robina, José, 'Estadística sobre defunciones por epilepsia', in *Actas del IX Congreso Internacional de Higiene y Demografía*, vol. 12, pp. 308–19.

Folley, Terence T., 'Some considerations of the religious allusions in Pérez Galdós' *Torquemada* novels', *Anales Galdosianos*, XIII (1978), 41–8.

Foucault, Michel, *Madness and Civilization: A History of Insanity in the Age of Reason* (London: Routledge, 1992).

Fuentes Peris, Teresa, *Images of Filth: Deviancy and Social Control in the Novels of Galdós* (Liverpool: Liverpool University Press, 2003).

Gallego y Gallego, Tomás, 'Mortalidad comparada de Europa', in *Actas y Memorias del IX Congreso Internacional de Higiene y Demografía*, vol 13, pp. 60–68.

Galton, Francis, Presidential address to the VII Congress of Hygiene and Demography, 11 August 1891, in *Transactions of the Seventh International Congress of Hygiene and Demography*. London, 10–17 August 1891. Ed. by C. E. Shelly. 13 vols (Eyre and Spottiswoode: London, 1892), vol. 10, pp. 7–12.

García Faria, Pedro, 'Fomento de la vitalidad en España', in *Actas del IX Congreso Internacional de Higiene y Demografía*, vol. 13, pp. 46–50.

Giné y Partagás, Juan, *Curso elemental de higiene privada y pública*, 4 vols (Barcelona: Imprenta de Narciso Ramírez y Cñía, 1872).

—— 'El idiotismo o imbecilidad moral. Discurso pronunciado en la sesión inaugural del "Ateneo Graciense"', celebrada el día 12 de octubre de 1895', in *Obras escogidas* (Barcelona: Tipografía la Académica, 1903), pp. 529–45.

—— *Tratado teórico-práctico de Freno-patología, ó Estudio de las enfermedades mentales fundado en la Clínica y en la fisiología de los centros nerviosos* (Madrid: E. Cuesta, 1876).

Giner de los Ríos, Francisco. 'La prohibición de la mendicidad y las Hermanitas de los Pobres', *Boletín de la Institución Libre de Enseñanza*, 5 (1881), 49–50.

Goldman, Peter B., 'Galdós and the politics of reconciliation', *Anales Galdosianos*, IV (1969), 74–87.

González Alvarez, Baldomero, 'Higiene profiláctica del niño respecto a la herencia', *El Siglo Médico*, 50 (30 August 1903), 582–5.

Gullón, Ricardo, *Galdós, novelista moderno* (Madrid: Gredos, 1960).

Hall, H. B., 'Torquemada: The man and his language', in J. E. Varey (ed.), *Galdós Studies* (London: Tamesis, 1970), pp. 136–63.

Hardy, A. and Charcot, J. M., *Informe de los doctores A. Hardy y J. M. Charcot [. . .] respecto del estado mental de D. Martín Larios y Larios* (Madrid: Est. Tipográfico Sucesores de Rivadeneyra, 1889).

Harris, Jose, 'Between civic virtue and Social Darwinism: The concept of the residuum', in David Englander and Rosemary O'Day (eds), *Retrieved Riches: Social Investigation in Britain* (Aldershot: Scolar Press, 1995), pp. 67–87.

Hauser, Philippe, *Madrid bajo el punto de vista médico-social*, 2 vols (Madrid: Establecimiento Tipográfico Sucesores de Rivadeneyra, 1902).

—— 'El siglo XIX considerado bajo el punto de vista médico-social', *Revista de España*, 101 (1884), 202–24, 333–58.

Hoar, Leo, 'More on the pre- (and post-) history of the *Episodios Nacionales*: Galdós' article "El dos de mayo" (1874)', *Anales Galdosianos*, VIII (1973), 107–20.

Hobson, J. A., *Imperialism: A Study* (1902).

Hollander, Stanley, *The Economics of John Stuart Mill* (Oxford: Blackwell, 1985).

Honderich, Ted (ed.), *The Oxford Companion to Philosophy*, 2nd edn (Oxford: Oxford University Press, 2005).

Huertas, Rafael, 'Valentín Magnan y la teoría de la degeneración', *Revista de la Asociación Española de Neuropsiquiatría*, V, 14 (1985), 361–7.

Huizinga, Meno, 'Rapport sur les dangers auxquels est exposé le système nerveux des écoliers et des étudiants par l'application qu'exigent les études et les examens; et sur les moyens d'y remédier', in *Cinquième Congrès international d'hygiène et de démographie* à La Haye, vol. 2, pp. 94–105.

Iglesias y Díaz, Manuel, 'Causas que contribuyen a la mortalidad de los niños. Medios de remediarlas. Estadísticas comparativas', in *Actas del IX Congreso Internacional de Higiene y Demografía*, vol. 6, pp. 9–20.

Jagoe, Catherine, Alda Blanco and Cristina Enríquez de Salamanca, *La mujer en los discursos de género: Textos y contextos en el siglo XIX* (Barcelona: Icaria, 1998).

Kirsner, Robert, 'Pérez Galdós' vision of Spain in *Torquemada en la hoguera*', *Bulletin of Hispanic Studies*, 27 (1950), 229–35.

Kuborn, H., 'De l'influence des programmes scolaires sur la santé des enfants', in *Quatrième Congrès international d'hygiène et de démographie à Genève*, vol. 2, pp. 381–401.

Labanyi, Jo, *Gender and Modernization in the Spanish Realist Novel* (Oxford: Oxford University Press, 2000).

Labra, Rafael María de, 'El esfuerzo individual' (Discurso pronunciado en la inauguración del Curso Académico de 1878–79, del Ateneo Mercantil de Madrid. Octubre de 1878), in *Discursos políticos, académicos y forenses* (Primera Serie) (Madrid: Imprenta de Aurelio J. Alaria, 1884), pp. 203–16.

Laín Sorrosal, Pedro, 'Causas que contribuyen a la mortalidad de los niños, y medio de remediarlas', in *Actas del IX Congreso Internacional de Higiene y Demografía*, vol 6, pp. 51–65.

Lida, Denah, 'Galdós y sus santas modernas', *Anales Galdosianos*, X (1975), 19–31.

López Piñero, José María, *Los orígenes históricos del concepto de neurosis* (Valencia: Cátedra e Instituto de Historia de la Medicina, 1963).

Malo, Bernabé, 'Causas que contribuyen a la mortalidad de los niños. Medios de remediarlas. Estadísticas comparativas', in *Actas del IX Congreso Internacional de Higiene y Demografía*, vol. 6, pp. 38–51.

Maristanyi, Luis, 'Lombroso y España: Nuevas consideraciones', *Anales de Literatura Española*, 2 (1983), Universidad de Alicante, 361–81.

Martínez Vargas, Andrés, *Nuestras madres y el engrandecimiento patrio* (Barcelona: Establecimiento Tipográfico de Jaime Vives, 1906).

Minter, Gordon, 'The medical background to Galdós' *La desheredada*', *Anales Galdosianos*, VII (1972), 67–77.

Morán, Valentín, 'Conferencias para obreros', *Revista de la Sociedad Económica Matritense*, 5 (1879), 28–31.

Muñoz Ruiz de Pasanis, Antonio, *Alcoholismo: su influencia en la degeneración de la raza latina* (Madrid: Ginés Carrión, 1906).

Nead, Lynda, *Myths of Sexuality: Representations of Women in Victorian Britain* (Oxford: Basil Blackwell, 1990).

Nimetz, Michael, *Humor in Galdós* (New Haven and London: Yale University Press, 1968).

O'Brien, Mac Gregor, 'Las religiones de Torquemada', *Discurso Literario*, 9, 2 (1985), 111–19.

Pérez Bautista, Florencio L., *El tema de la enfermedad en la novela realista española* (Salamanca: Ediciones del Instituto de Historia de la Medicina Española, 1972).

Perrot, Michelle (ed.), *A History of Private Life*, IV: *From the Fires of Revolution to the Great War* (Cambridge, Mass.: Belknap Press of Harvard University Press, 1990).

Peset, José Luis and Mariano Peset, *Lombroso y la escuela positivista italiana* (Madrid: C.S.I.C., 1975).

Peseux-Richard, H., Review of *Torquemada y San Pedro*, in *Review Hispanique*, 2 (1895), 197–8.

Pick, Daniel, *Faces of Degeneration* (Cambridge: Cambridge University Press, 1993).

Portero, José Antonio, *Púlpito e ideología en la España del siglo XIX* (Zaragoza: Libros Pórtico, 1978).

Prochaska, Frank, *Women and Philanthropy in Nineteenth-Century England* (Oxford: Clarendon Press, 1980).

—— *The Voluntary Impulse: Philanthropy in Modern Britain* (London: Faber & Faber, 1988).

Programme du VI congrès international d'hygiène et de démographie (du 26 septembre au 2 octobre 1887), Vienne, 1887.

Quatrième Congrès international d'hygiène et de démographie à Genève (du 4 au 9 septembre 1882). Comptes rendus et mémoires publiés par P.-L. Dunant. 2 tomes, Genève, 1883.

Rey González, Antonio M. (ed.), *Estudios médico-sociales sobre marginados en la España del siglo XIX* (Madrid: Ministerio de Sanidad y Consumo, 1990).

Sánchez Barbudo, Antonio, 'Torquemada y la muerte' *Anales Galdosianos*, II (1967), 45–52.

Sánchez Rubio, E., *Bibliographie espagnole d'Hygiène et de Démographie*, in *Actas del IX Congreso Internacional de Higiene y Demografía*, vol. 12, pp. 31–55.

Santero, Francisco Javier, *Elementos de higiene privada y pública*, 2 vols (Madrid: El Cosmos, 1885).

Sanz, Timoteo, 'Problemas médico-sociales: Regenerados y degenerados', in *El Siglo Médico*, 39 (14 August 1892), 519.

Sarabia y Pardo, Jesús, *El suicidio como enfermedad social* (Madrid: Publicaciones de la Sociedad Española de Higiene, 1889).

Scanlon, Geraldine, '*El doctor Centeno*: A study in obsolescent values', *Bulletin of Hispanic Studies*, LV, 3 (1978), 245–53.

—— *Pérez Galdós: Marianela* (Critical Guides to Spanish Texts) (London: Tamesis, 1988).

—— 'Torquemada: "Becerro de oro"', *Modern Language Notes*, 91, 1 (1976), 264–76.

Schyfter, Sara E., *The Jew in the Novels of Benito Pérez Galdós* (London: Tamesis, 1978).

Sherzer, William M., 'Death and succession in the *Torquemada* series', *Anales Galdosianos*, XIII (1978), 33–9.

Shirley, Paula W., 'Religious contexts in the Torquemada novels', *Hispanófila*, 29, 2 (1986), 67–73.

Showalter, Elaine, *The Female Malady: Women, Madness and English Culture, 1830–1980* (London: Virago, 1987).

Sikorsky, Dr, 'Contribution à l'étude des maladies nerveuses chez les enfants à l'âge scolaire', in *Quatrième Congrès international d'hygiène et de démographie à Genève*, vol. 2, pp. 453–5.

Sinnigen, John, H., 'Literary and ideological projects in Galdós: The *Torquemada* series', *Ideologies and Literature*, 3, 11 (1979), 5–19.

Smiles, Samuel, ¡*Ayúdate*! (Barcelona: Ramón Sopena). Tr. by G. Nuñez de Prado. (Undated)

—— *El carácter*. Tr. by Emilio Soulère (Paris: Garnier Hermanos, 1892).

—— *Los hombres de energía y coraje: Notas biográficas tomadas del popular libro titulado 'Self-help'* (Madrid: Imprenta de Aurelio J. Alaria, 1876).

—— *Self-Help* (London: John Murray, 1958) (Originally published in 1859).

Snape, Robert, 'Betting, billiards and smoking: leisure in public libraries', *Leisure Studies*, 11 (1992), 187–99.

Summers, Anne, 'A home from home – women's philanthropic work in the nineteenth century', in Sandra Burman (ed.), *Fit Work for Women* (London: Croom Helm, 1979), pp. 33–63.

Tolosa Latour, Manuel, 'Concepto y fines de la higiene popular', in *Discursos leídos en la Real Academia de Medicina para la recepción pública del académico electo Manuel de Tolosa Latour* (Madrid: Est. Tip. de la viuda e hijos de Tello, 1900), pp. 7–43.

—— *Medicina e higiene de los niños* (Madrid: Biblioteca Científica Moderna, 1893).

Trinidad Fernández, Pedro, 'La reforma de las cárceles en el siglo XIX: las cárceles de Madrid', in *Estudios de Historia Social*, 22–23 (1982), 69–187.

Urey, Diane, 'Identities and differences in the *Torquemada* novels of Galdós', in Jo Labanyi (ed.), *Galdós* (London, Longman, 1993), pp. 181–98. Reprinted from *Hispanic Review*, 53 (1985).

Valera y Jiménez, Tomás, 'La salud nacional es la riqueza nacional', *El Siglo Médico*, 39 (13 November 1892), 732–5.

La Voz de la caridad (various issues).

'A way to clean rivers', *Household Words*, XVIII (10 July 1858), 79–82.

Weber, Robert J., 'Galdós's preliminary sketches for *Torquemada y San Pedro*', *Bulletin of Hispanic Studies*, 44 (1967), 16–27.

Index